UNIVERSITY

W9-AUL-214

ERNISM, MEDICINE, AND WILLIAM CARLOS WILLIAMS

Oklahoma Project for
Discourse and Theory
The Series for Science and Culture

Modernism, Medicine, & William Carlos Williams

by T. Hugh Crawford

University of Oklahoma Press : Norman and London

On the title page: William Carlos Williams, M.D., bending over microscope. University of Pennsylvania Medical School, class of 1906. (Courtesy of The University of Pennsylvania Archives)

Library of Congress Cataloging-in-Publication Data

Crawford, T. Hugh (Thomas Hugh), 1956–
    Modernism, medicine & William Carlos Williams / by T. Hugh Crawford.
        p.   cm — (Oklahoma project for discourse and theory)
    Includes bibliographical references (p.) and index.
    ISBN 0–8061–2550–0 (alk. paper)
        1. Williams, William Carlos, 1883–1963—Criticism and interpretation.
    2. Modernism (Literature)—United States.   3. Literature and medicine.
    4. Medicine in literature. I. Title. II. Title: Modernism, medicine, and William Carlos Williams. III. Series.
    PS3545.I544Z5835   1993
    811'.52—dc20   93–19161
                                                                    CIP

Modernism, Medicine, and William Carlos Williams is Volume 1 of the Oklahoma Project for Discourse and Theory: The Series for Science and Culture.

The paper in this book meets the guidelines for permanence and durability of the Committee on Production Guidelines for Book Longevity of the Council on Library Resources, Inc. ∞

Contents

Illustrations

On the title page: William Carlos Williams, M.D., bending over microscope. University of Pennsylvania Medical School, class of 1906.

Editors' Foreword

Since its inception in 1987, the Oklahoma Project for Discourse and Theory has challenged and helped to redefine the boundaries of traditional disciplinary structures of knowledge. Employing various approaches, ranging from feminism and deconstruction to sociology and nuclear studies, books in this series have offered their readers opportunities to explore our postmodern condition. In the Series on Science and Culture, the Oklahoma Project extends its inquiries into the postdisciplinary areas of the complex relations among the humanities, social sciences, and sciences. The term *postdisciplinary* is meant to suggest that we have entered an era of rapid sociocultural and technological change in which "common sense" divisions between, say, physics and literature no longer seem as sensible as they once did. The values and assumptions, methods and technologies, that we had been taught were "natural" and "universal" are being challenged, reworked, and demystified to demonstrate the ways in which they are culturally constructed. All coherence may not be gone, but what counts as coherence is being redefined in provocative ways.

In recent years, the study of science, both within and outside of the academy, has undergone a sea change. Traditional approaches to the history and philosophy of science treated science as an insular set of procedures concerned to reveal fundamental truths or laws of the physical universe. In contrast, the postdisciplinary study of science emphasizes its cultural embeddedness, the ways in which particular laboratories, experiments, instruments, scientists, and procedures are historically and socially situated. Science is no longer a closed system that generates carefully plotted paths proceeding asymptotically towards the truth, but an open system that is everywhere penetrated by contingent and even competing accounts of what constitutes our world. These include—but are by no means limited to—the discourses of race, gender, social class, politics, theology, anthropology, sociology, and literature. In the phrase of Nobel laureate Ilya Prigogine, we have moved from a science of being to a science of becoming. This becoming is the ongoing concern of the volumes in the Series on Science and Culture. Their purpose is to open up possibilities for further inquiries rather than to close off debate.

The members of the editorial board of the series reflect our commitment to reconceiving the structures of knowledge. All are prominent in their fields, although in every case what their "field" is has been redefined, in large measure by their own work. The departmental or program affiliations of these distinguished scholars—Sander Gilman, Donna Haraway, N. Katherine Hayles, Bruno Latour, Richard Lewontin, Michael Morrison, Mark Poster, G. S. Rousseau, and Donald Worster—seem to tell us less about what they do than where, institutionally, they have been. Taken together as a set of strategies for rethinking the relationships between science and culture, their work exemplifies the kind of careful, self-critical scrutiny within fields such as medicine, biology, anthropology, history, physics, and literary criticism that leads us to a recognition of the limits of what and how we have been taught to think. The postdisciplinary aspects of our board members' work stem from their professional expertise within their home disciplines and their willingness to expand their studies to other, seemingly alien fields. In differing ways, their work challenges the basic divisions within western thought between metaphysics and physics, mind and body, form and matter.

ROBERT MARKLEY

University of Washington

ROBERT CON DAVIS
RONALD SCHLEIFER

University of Oklahoma

Acknowledgments

For their help in the early stages of this project, I would like to thank Bernard Duffey, John Leland, and Frank Lentricchia. In addition, I thank the National Endowment for the Humanities for Summer Institutes at Tufts and Columbia Universities, and the Virginia Military Institute Research Laboratories for defraying the cost of travel to collections. For their assistance in the final manuscript preparation, I thank William D. Badgett, Yolanda Warren, Tim Spence, Larry Hamberlin, and, most importantly, Richard Grusin.

Parts of chapters 1 and 7 appeared in different form in *Medicine and Literature* and *The William Carlos Williams Review.*

This book is dedicated to Dr. William B. Crawford, who showed me what it means to be a doctor, and to Maria Gregory Crawford, who showed me what it means to have patience.

MODERNISM, MEDICINE, AND WILLIAM CARLOS WILLIAMS

Abbreviations

A   *The Autobiography of William Carlos Williams*
BU   *The Build-Up*
CP1   *The Collected Poems of William Carlos Williams,* vol. 1, *1909–1939*
CP2   *The Collected Poems of William Carlos Williams,* vol. 2, *1939–1962*
DS   *The Doctor Stories*
EK   *The Embodiment of Knowledge*
FD   *The Farmers' Daughters*
I   *Imaginations*
IAG   *In The American Grain*
IM   *I Wanted to Write a Poem*
Int   *Interviews with William Carlos Williams*
JS   *William Carlos Williams/John Sanford: A Correspondence*
LNP   *Last Nights of Paris*
ML   *Many Loves and Other Plays*
P   *Paterson*
RI   *A Recognizable Image: William Carlos Williams on Art and Artists*
SE   *Selected Essays of William Carlos Williams*
SL   *The Selected Letters of William Carlos Williams*
VTP   *A Voyage to Pagany*
WM   *White Mule*
Y   *Yes, Mrs. Williams*

Introduction

It may have been my studies in medicine; it may have been my intense feeling of Americanism; anyhow I knew that I wanted reality in my poetry and I began to try to let it speak.
—I Wanted to Write a Poem

This new tinge to modern minds is a vehement and passionate interest in the relation of general principles to irreducible and stubborn facts.
—Alfred North Whitehead

The origin of potency lies in confusion: it is no longer possible to distinguish an actor from the allies which make it strong.
—Bruno Latour

William Carlos Williams's short story "Old Doc Rivers" begins with "Horses" and ends with the title character riding in an automobile on a housecall. Although Rivers's career predates Williams's own by nearly a generation, this shift in mode of transportation is emblematic of radical changes in the medical profession at the turn of the century and is symptomatic of broader social and cultural shifts in America at the beginning of what is called by literary historians the modern period. Williams was born in 1881 into the era of the steamship and horse and buggy, but he soon witnessed the birth of the modern city, the transportation revolution, and— because of the general acceptance of germ theory, laboratory medicine, aseptic practices, and publicly sponsored health programs— the emerging dominance of scientific medicine.[1] Consequently, his writing bears witness to the cultural authority science and tech-

3

nology held in the popular imagination of modern Americans. This book is not so much about William Carlos Williams as it is about that authority. It examines the strategies employed by one writer who attempted to carve out a place for himself in what, retrospectively, must be viewed as a time of massive cultural upheaval.

Williams was a child of the modern period and one of its most eloquent spokesmen, but a close look at his texts reveals not only his attempt to create a fresh American aesthetic but also his own private battle with the changes he was witnessing. This study will attempt an archaeology of modern American discourse—a dig that reveals shifts in epistemology characterizing this century and uncovers complex relationships between specific discursive practices. I am proposing that the cultural power of science and technology can be measured by the adoption of their vocabulary and epistemology by other discourses.[2] Williams developed his own form of modernism not so much from his contact with other important early modern figures (Ezra Pound, Wallace Stevens, Marianne Moore) as from his medical and scientific studies. Those studies were not only sources for Williams's literary ideals but also strategies used to claim authority to speak at a time when widely divergent voices competed for attention in the literary marketplace. As modernism became institutionalized, however, Williams began to question both its authority and the cultural power of technoscientific discourses in general—a questioning that lead him toward a form of postmodernism.

In 1902, upon graduating from Horace Mann High School in New York City, Williams began his medical studies at the University of Pennsylvania. It was a time of significant change in medicine. A degree could no longer be obtained through a short apprenticeship, and soon most medical schools would require a college degree for admission. By 1910 the American Medical Association had achieved hard-won hegemony,[3] and, because of the spectacular success of Louis Pasteur, Joseph Lister, Robert Koch, and others, the influence of the French clinical method (primarily promulgated by students of Pierre Louis) was being displaced by laboratory practices. Charles Eliot began restructuring Harvard's medical school along scientific lines in 1871, and Johns Hopkins Medical School, which placed strong emphasis on laboratory work and became the model for twentieth-century medical education, opened its doors in 1893. In other words, American medical education and (to a lesser degree) practice were becoming increasingly scientific.[4]

That shift, typified by Sir William Osler's frequent discussions of the relation of medicine to science and art, achieved broad acceptance with the publication of Abraham Flexner's famous *Report to the Carnegie Foundation* in 1910. The ideas contained in Flexner's report (which were to become the basis for scientific medical education in America) were already very much in the air in the years before 1906, when Williams graduated from the University of Pennsylvania Medical School.[5] Williams completed his own education in Leipzig (his peers in the middle nineteenth century would have studied in Edinburgh or Paris), but after his return from Germany, he took up what could only be characterized as a rural (later suburban) practice in his hometown, Rutherford, New Jersey. Like Old Doc Rivers, professionally Williams was caught between two worlds—the doctor trained in laboratory technique and the rural practitioner who depended on the uncertain effects of an "unscientific" pharmacopeia and on *vis medicatrix naturae*.

The modern period was a time of great change for both of Williams's professions—medicine and writing—and his attitude toward the relationship between the two is problematic. In his 1951 autobiography he comments, "When they ask me, as of late they frequently do, how I have for so many years continued an equal interest in medicine and the poem, I reply that they amount for me to nearly the same thing."[6] Although there is much self-assurance in that statement, anyone familiar with Williams's work will note that, rather than a sense of identity between the two "lives," there is a continual rolling of emotion about one relative to the other. Their relationship has sparked numerous psychological interpretations about the effect medical practice had on his work.[7] Williams's own comments often give a sense of absolute division between the two professions. In *Kora in Hell* (1920) he notes, "The trick is never to touch the world anywhere. Leave yourself at the door, walk in, admire the pictures, talk a few words with the master of the house, question his wife a little, rejoin yourself at the door—and go off arm in arm listening to last week's symphony played by angel hornsmen from the benches of a turned cloud" (*I* 53). It is fairly easy to propose psychological explanations for this self-protective distancing, and, given the particulars of Williams's medical practice as it is described in his texts, his need to protect his middle-class sensibility through such distancing is not surprising.

What is significant about this image of the doctor as part partici-pant, part voyeur, however, is its role as the linchpin of Williams's poetics. The disengagement lauded here is that of both the aesthete and the objective scientist; at the same time, it was a position Wil-liams could never maintain. In the years just following the publica-tion of *Kora in Hell* he developed (along with Robert McAlmon) his doctrine of "contact"—a position that completely contradicts the above quotation.

Williams's voyeuristic aesthetic does raise the epistemological issue of both science and writing: bounded space.[8] Modern sci-ence is concerned with bounding experience and unveiling objects in order to produce knowledge. (These ideas are explored in chap-ters 2 and 3.) In order to understand both scientific and cultural authority, one must know how lines are drawn and space policed. The inside and the outside are crucial positions occupied by the narrators of Williams's texts and the texts themselves, so follow-ing the trajectory of these lines through the various discourses that allow them to be drawn is a fundamental first move. Williams's discussion of medical school in *The Autobiography* examines his conflicting attitudes toward medicine and writing while, at the same time, showing his reticence about the modernization of America. He knew he wanted to be a poet but wanted to please his family. After toying with joining the theater, he settled on medicine: "It was money that finally decided me. I would continue medicine, for I was determined to be a poet; only medicine, a job I enjoyed, would make it possible for me to live and write as I wanted to. I would live: that first, and write, by God, as *I* wanted to if it took me all eternity to accomplish my design" (*A* 51). Williams's anx-iety manifests itself on a deeper level than the psychic need for fulfillment and an economically stable home life. It runs to the problem of medicine and art as a commodity. In *A Voyage to Pagany* Dev Evans abuses (under his breath) his fellow American practi-tioners who have come to Vienna to study new pediatric methods. "Come here to feed, to fill up in order to disgorge at a stiff price later; at their best, good only to acquire some skill which, as they turn it into cash, they do something of value with it, or at least keep themselves from doing harm" (*VTP* 148). Leaving aside for the moment the point that Williams, the militant antitraditionalist, is siding with the old institution against the new and decidedly American approach to medicine, this diatribe shows his nostalgia for a golden age of medicine, an age of altruism before the consolidation of the AMA and advanced capitalism.[9]

His nostalgia for the art of medicine and the art of poetry working under a different mode of production is often covered by a brash, almost mercenary attitude, but his bitterness in *The Autobiography* about his own publishing history and his only relative success as a physician in measurable (monetary) terms betrays his dissatisfaction. Williams's estrangement from art has been discussed in some detail in Bernard Duffey's *Poetry of Presence.*[10] Williams was an outsider to his fellow poets because he was a doctor. He was an outsider to his fellow townspeople because he was a poet. He was an outsider to his lower-class patients because he was a doctor (and therefore educated) and a poet (to those aware of that fact). Finally, he was an outsider to poetry because he was an American and the literature of the time was European even if written by American expatriates. Consequently, he can be seen as a poetic *bricoleur* using what voices, forms, and languages he can in his assault on a stale tradition or a misguided modernism. Ironically, one of the sources of his alienation—his medical training—leads him to desire poetic radicalism and in the process offers him both discursive and epistemological authority.

An understanding of the relation of medicine to Williams's texts prepares the way for a broader historical and sociological analysis of the discursive power of science. It can be objected that Williams's texts show little knowledge of the philosophy and history of medicine. Nevertheless, because of his training (in medical school and American society), he was a member of what Ludwik Fleck calls a "thought collective," and consequently perceived the world in a fairly circumscribed fashion. In *The Genesis and Development of a Scientific Fact,* Fleck defines a "thought style" as a conditioned way of perceiving and conceptualizing data: "If we define 'thought collective' as *a community of persons mutually exchanging ideas or maintaining intellectual interaction, we will find by implication that it also provides a special "carrier" for the historical development of any field of thought, as well as for the given stock of knowledge and level of culture. This we have designated thought style.*"[11] Although one must be cautious when invoking any group as a stable entity (the middle class, scientists, society, etc.), Fleck's formulation shows how group behavior is conditioned by historically constituted ways of knowing. Williams was a member (however marginal) of a medical thought collective, and his literary texts (the product of another thought collective) show not only evidence of this style but also allow a glimpse into its history and contradictions.

Members of a thought collective have a readiness for *"directed perception, with corresponding mental and objective assimilation of what has been so perceived."* [12] Nevertheless, thought collectives are not totalitarian. They are coercive in that they guide perception and (in a sense) limit knowledge, but they also create the very possibility of knowledge (particularly as it is defined by a modern scientific epistemology). And, significantly, no one is governed by a single collective. Education (in the broadest sense of the term) imbues its subjects with numerous thought styles, and rarely does one completely dominate. Instead, participants in any collective bring with them other thought styles that jostle for power and, similar to Jean-François Lyotard's language games,[13] begin to bend the rules. Without doubt, Williams was initiated into a particular thought style while at the University of Pennsylvania and while practicing for forty years in Rutherford, Paterson, and Passaic, New Jersey. At the same time, his entire literary output was directed toward bending some (perceived) traditional rules, and those strategies often depended on his training in other styles— particularly the scientific collective.

This study examines the permutations of two specific and remarkably common concepts in Williams's writing, in medical texts, and in the discourse of modernism in general: clarity and cleanliness. From a medical perspective, the need for clarity of vision (or touch, taste, and smell) historically has been set up against systematic or rationalized medicine and achieved its highest epistemological status in the nineteenth century with the French clinical method. Cleanliness was also elevated in the nineteenth century through the public health movement (typified by Edwin Chadwick's *Report on the Sanitary Conditions of the Labouring Population of Great Britain* [1842] and Florence Nightingale's hospital design reforms), but it achieved full rhetorical power at the turn of the century with the general acceptance of germ theory. These two tropes, clarity and cleanliness, have a long history in both medical texts and in science in general, and they provide a way of understanding Williams's texts. Conversely, those texts help reveal the rhetorical power of the tropes.

Williams uses the central tenets of an emerging scientific hegemony in order to gain power to speak as a poet. As he associates with that power, he also aligns himself with its problems—problems that have been critiqued in some detail in the past few decades.[14] Science and technology occupy a different position of power in the early twentieth century than they do later (particularly after the popularization of relativity theory and the explosion of the atomic bomb), and Williams's own writing reflects some of the anxieties others began to feel about the authoritarian nature of science's practices. The final chapter of this book explores a shift in Williams's use of scientific and technological authority in his later writings, one that can be characterized as a movement from modernism to postmodernism.

This notion of historical periodization raises one final problem that needs discussion before turning to medical history and Williams's texts. Although it is pragmatically possible to invoke science or medicine as a thought style (and given science's drive for universality, this style *should* be fairly easy to define), one must be exceedingly cautious in using such categories uncritically. To steal a subtitle from one of Michel Foucault's books, this is an archaeology of medical perception, but the site of the dig is a different continent and one of the artifacts to be examined is the category of medicine. Foucault's brilliant analysis of the French clinical method takes as its premise the accomplished fact of science's hegemony by the late nineteenth century. Although he undercuts science's authority at every turn, the technologies developed in *The Birth of the Clinic* come to totalitarian authority in *Discipline and Punish*. Given that vision, one can talk about modernism and (possibly) postmodernism. Definitions for both of these periods, however, usually depend on science and technology's unquestioned ability to universalize data—a view that dominates most social critiques of science today. Although the ideas of the Frankfurt school, the Edinburgh school, the feminist critique of science, and the literature and science movement are important influences on this book, it is crucial not to take science's hegemony as a given. We should not naïvely become, in Bruno Latour's words, "wildly scientistic."

In *The Pasteurization of France* and "Give Me a Laboratory and I Will Shake the World," Bruno Latour examines the fundamental concept of modern science—reproducibility. For Latour, scientific facts depend not on their measure against nature as final arbiter but rather on their production at particular sites—laboratories. Pasteur produced scientific truth by inventing a portable laboratory that could, through standardized and routinized procedures, reproduce specific effects. Therefore, scientific facts are produced by networks, not by decoding nature: "So you believe that the application of mathematics to the physical world is a miracle? If so, then I invite you to admire another miracle; I can travel around the world with my American Express card. You say of the second, 'That's just a network. If you step out of it by so much as an inch, your card will be valueless.' Quite so. This is what I am saying about mathematics and science, *nothing more and nothing less.*"[15]

Latour's critique casts considerable doubt on the basis of science's authority in our culture. If scientific facts are the products of fragile networks, then scientists are not necessarily describing the effects of a possibly decodable nature or details with universal applicability.[16] Without universality, no true authority. Latour's work questions fundamentally the notion that any significant epistemological break from the past has occurred and, in a sense, forestalls any discussion of modernism or postmodernism.[17] But at the same time, he raises an important question: if science becomes universal through routinized procedures, how do we account for its power in our society? I hope in this study to show that scientific authority depends, not simply on the description of objects or networks of laboratories, but also on linguistic networks that create specific epistemologies; that this network is intertwined with other social networks; and that these networks are fragile and apt to disintegrate with the slightest pressure. Even if the authority of science is built on false principles,[18] its power—as measured by its discursive authority in the popular imagination—still constructs categories and shapes attitudes. We must invoke categories in order to discuss their effects and examine divisions in order to understand their power, but we can never take for granted their ontological security.

Williams's work can be viewed as a node through which pass numerous overlapping lines of force—poetry, modernism, science, medicine, technology, aesthetics, gender, and visual arts. They create a network that is strengthened through various associations. By examining the trajectory of these lines of force, we can begin to understand the node (Williams's work) and, at the same time, come to understand the functioning of the networks.

Authority, Honesty, and Charisma

You cannot write a prescription without the element of placebo. A prayer to Jupiter starts the prescription. It carries weight, the weight of two or three thousand years of medicine.

—Eugene F. DuBois

Truth is defined by those professionally certified to name it.

—C. S. Pierce

Mr. Eliot . . . seems to "sometimes" think that minds elaborately equipped with specific information, like science always must confuse it with other specific information, like poetry. That may be the case with unfortunates. The point, however, would be not to proffer solemnly or whiningly confusions to the confused, but to indicate by energetic mental behavior how certain information may be useful to other information, and when the divisions which signalize them are necessary.

—Louis Zukofsky

Until the health crisis of the 1970s, medicine was the most respected and lucrative profession of the twentieth century, a point not difficult to imagine given the tremendous technical advances in medical care (today surgery without anaesthesia is unimaginable) and the generalized positivism of the times. Doctors had always been masters of a hidden body of knowledge, dispensing arcane truths in such a way that people were often cured. By the turn of the century, they had also mastered the microbe, more or less. Germ theory, aseptic surgery, professionalized hospitals, and an increasingly effective pharmacopeia not only raised respect for the medical profession but also rarefied its knowledge and reified its practitioners. In a society increasingly enamored of science and technology, the medical profession's rise to the status of sovereign profession[1] seems inevitable.

Through the centuries esteem for physicians has fluctuated drastically, and since medicine relies on the confidence of its patients perhaps even more than it does its own skills, it is not surprising to see in medical discourse a concern for establishing and maintaining authority. Under normal circumstances, doctors cannot force their patients to take a prescribed treatment. Consequently, much of their training is not simply scientific; it is also rhetorical. Even a casual look at older medical treatises demonstrates an interest in the social power of discourse. In the *Prognostics* Hippocrates discusses the importance of accurate prognosis, which, one would assume, is necessary for successful treatment, particularly in acute cases. Nevertheless, Hippocrates' discussion focuses on the doctor's self-presentation: "Thus a man will be the more esteemed to be a good physician, for he will be the better able to treat those aright who can be saved, from having long anticipated everything; and by seeing and announcing beforehand those who will live and those who will die, he will thus escape censure."[2] Hippocrates' concern here is primarily for the patient, yet he ends not with the doctor-patient relationship but with the doctor's professional and social standing.

Galen provides another instance of this concern in *De locis affectis,* where he recalls a spectacular diagnosis during his first visit to Rome. The case history contains the information necessary for a student of medicine (at the time) to diagnose cirrhosis and therefore fulfills its ostensible purpose. Nevertheless, Galen does not emphasize the actual points of diagnosis. Instead, he describes how he deceived the two doctors involved—the patient (who was a physician) and the doctor attending. With the glee of a murder mystery detective, he recounts the details he scrupulously noted to make the diagnosis, including in particular the bedpan containing "a thin sanio-sanguinolent fluid, in which floated excrementitious masses that resembled shreds of flesh."[3] Galen's case history makes two important points, beyond its diagnostic value. He demonstrates that diagnosis is not a black art or divinely inspired but rather is the result of detailed, objective observation. He demystifies the art of medicine for those who are reading the document and are therefore presumably studying medicine. But at the same time he teaches those same students the art of *re*mystification. He points to the exact spot where the patient feels pain but does not tell him or the attending physician how he came to such knowledge. Galen passes off his diagnosis as something divine and gleefully asserts in closing, "Glaucon's confidence in me and in the medical art, after this episode, was unbounded."[4] Even in Galen's time, medicine was an art of concealing as well as revealing. Doctors provide just enough information to effect change and enhance their reputation, but at the same time, they maintain an air of mystery and glory in the power it brings.

In nineteenth-century America there were numerous competing medical sects, each of whom would readily impugn the character of the other to further its own following. The profession had difficulty borrowing authority from older forms because, in the United States, institutionalized power was regarded with suspicion. Geographically people were dispersed, and they endured hardships; sickness was simply one among many. Therefore, Yankee self-reliance was extended to medical matters, and self-cure dominated. Many people relied on home remedy books such as John C. Gunn's *Domestic Medicine,* which professes on its title page to be "In Plain Language, Free from Doctor's Terms . . . Intended Expressly for the Benefit of Families . . . Arranged on a New Simple Plan, By Which the Practice of Medicine Is Reduced to Principles of Common Sense."[5] This appeal to simplicity, common sense, and openness is a powerful rhetoric in the American tradition. It was difficult for the medical profession to overcome the popular attitude that medicine, like interpreting the Bible or choosing a government, was an individual matter.

William Carlos Williams became a doctor at precisely the time when medicine changed from one of the least desirable of the professions (for the upper middle class) to the most respected. The late nineteenth century witnessed the reform of established medical education, which brought about stricter licensing measures and drove many proprietary medical schools out of business. In 1901 the AMA reviewed its charter and changed its requirements on the state level, expanding its membership from eight thousand in 1900 to seventy thousand in 1910.[6] Physicians now controlled hospital privileges and referrals, and they instituted a code of ethics that resembles a code of silence. In the space of thirty years American medicine was transformed from a hack profession anyone with one or two years' education or an apprenticeship could enter to an exclusive club that rigorously controlled both the admittance and the behavior of its members. These medical initiates were privy to the sacred and henceforth generally unavailable truth of health.

It is of some consequence that Williams belonged to two professions concerned with clearly established authority. In *Spring and All* he unites his poetic sensibility and medical knowledge to attack those who do not understand art: "The reason people marvel at works of art and say: How in Christ's name did he do it?—is that they know nothing of the physiology of the nervous system and have never in their experience witnessed the larger processes of the imagination" (*I* 123). He invokes his expertise in physiology—a field in which few are trained—and his own "larger processes of the imagination," which are demonstrated by the book that contains this passage. Both are strategies for gaining authority to speak a truth in a given context.[7] Trained in a profession designed to make utterances a matter of life and death, Williams chose literature as his second profession, a practice that foregrounds the difficulty of finding a position from which to speak. His alter ego Dr. Paterson

> envies the men that ran
> and could run off
> toward the peripheries—
> to other centers, direct—
> for clarity (if
> they found it)
>   loveliness and
> authority in the world—
>   (*Paterson* 36)

Though *Paterson* is more tentative in its expression of authority than some of Williams's earlier work (a point discussed in chapter 8), here he expresses the need for a point on which to stand in order to utter a truth. One source of clarity (which brings with it authority) is the medical scene, a place Williams visited as a physician almost daily. Consequently, it is not surprising to find in his writing the scene of medical pronouncement and to see parallel concerns for literature's authority to produce similar truths.

His early short story "Mind and Body" examines in detail these issues. It opens as a monologue—a disembodied voice. The reader must infer the medical scene, as the doctor does not speak for several paragraphs. The patient attacks specific doctors and medicine in general. The doctor, polite and restrained, lets her tell her story and in the process reveal her above-average education and intelligence. She has a degree from Cornell, can discuss Caesar's commentaries, and has worked as an executive secretary and a nurse. In other words, not only is she the potential intellectual equal of a man who deals most of the time with ignorant immigrants,[8] she is also an initiate in the medical profession. The doctor must either locate her specific problem (she seems to be a hypochondriac) or offer exegesis of a text above her level. As in Galen's case study where the patient was another doctor, "Mind and Body" establishes this patient as a formidable opponent.

The case history here is significant. Not only does the reader learn about the failure of other doctors and drugs in specific treatments, he or she also discovers that there is insanity in the family, the patient is an atheist, and she holds many of Williams's own ideas (writing needs to have some music in it and college ruins originality in youth). The narrator's pose in drawing out the case history plays a key role. Other doctors are classified by the patient as fools, so he adopts reticence: his first break into the monologue is prefaced with "I ventured to ask" (*FD* 39). The story is a script for dealing with such a patient: let her talk herself out. The doctor gains authority by not overcommitting himself and instead saves his words for strategic attack. He casually mentions Socrates, which pleases his patient, but then his examination fails to locate her problem. She attacks; he becomes defensive and then obfuscates, first with Greek uterine lore, then mucous colitis,[9] and finally with capillaroscopy: "The anatomic basis for your condition, I continued, seems to have been detected in a new study called capillaroscopy, a study of the microscopic terminal blood vessels. In people of your type these terminal loops between the arteries and the veins are long and gracile. They are frail, expand and contract easily, it is the cause of all the unstable nervous phenomena which you see" (*FD* 48). One has the sense that it is only the patient's education that keeps him from explaining her problems by the actions of the four humors. Nevertheless, the diagnosis (which here is the equivalent of a cure, since he does not prescribe treatment) is effected. The doctor, like Galen, can gleefully claim cure by mystification.

The irony of "Mind and Body" is precisely that of Galen's case history. While the story is a textbook case for an office examination and the writing of a patient's history (if one can overlook the chauvinism),[10] it is also nearly the exercise of power for power's sake and an example of professional dissembling. As Pliny says, "That whosoever professeth himself a physician, is straightwaies beleeved, say what he will: and yet to speake a truth, there are no lies dearer sold or more daungerous than those which proceed out of a Physician's mouth."[11] Williams's narrator cures by misnaming the disease hidden in the woman's abdomen, a "placebo" diagnosis that converts fear into acquiescence. Because one expects to be confused by medical jargon, the language of the doctor is, ironically, reassuring. Power, as Michel Foucault has argued, is exerted through the rarefaction of discourse.[12] "Fellowships of discourse" create a common vocabulary not commonly available. In "Mind and Body" the doctor must communicate something, even if that communication is willfully obscure or arcane.

A patient may be frightened by cancer, but the specificity of the words diagnosing the particular form of the disease furthers the illusion of the medical profession's knowledge of and ability to treat an individual illness. The act of naming the terror hidden in the body of a patient is the first step toward casting out the demon of the disease and must be recognized as a rhetorical power. The scene of this cure is not the laboratory, where noise is excluded or controlled to the point where one can attain a simple differential diagnosis—positive or negative. Instead, it is the physician's office, which has the trappings of a laboratory, but at the same time contains the tale as it is drawn out through the careful positioning of the narrator.

Although a bit scandalous, dissembling has long been a part of medicine's therapeutic arsenal and, in the case of placebos, can be quite effective. Nevertheless, dissembling often serves not the cause of the cure but rather the broader social authority of the physician. Arnauld of Villanova (1235?–1311) was one of the first physicians to write a handbook of professional deceit for the maintenance of cultural authority.[13] His text is clearly concerned with patients who, like the woman in "Mind and Body," attempt to test the physician's knowledge and abilities. Indeed, Williams's narrator could possibly have used Arnauld's advice in his diagnosis: "There is a seventh precaution, and it is a very general one; you may not find out anything about the case, then say he has an obstruction in the liver. He may say: 'No sir, on the contrary he has pains in the head, or in the legs or in other organs.' You must say that this comes from the liver or from the stomach; and particularly use the word, obstruction, because they do not understand what it means, and it helps greatly that a term is not understood by the people."[14] Capillaroscopy (or microangioscopy), a term not understood by the people, is a recognized procedure and not simply a construction by the narrator. What is significant in the story is not the accuracy of the doctor's diagnosis (which does remain questionable) but his calling upon a relatively obscure practice in order to give the patient a new term. She probably would not have accepted neurasthenia or mucous colitis as an accurate description of her malady, so the narrator gives her the most up-to-date diagnosis possible, even though its explanatory power is dubious at best.

In "Mind and Body" Williams demystifies medicine by exposing deliberate obfuscation. He shows the reader that doctors can be (as many have often suspected) duplicitous. Nevertheless, he gains authority to write the story precisely because he is one of those dissemblers. His medical training and practice give him the expertise to detail the scene and contribute to his rhetorical skill both within the events of the story and in its framing ("Mind and Body" can be read as an extended case history). Few readers can remain ignorant of Williams's profession, so, like the patient in the story, most must bow to the superior medical vocabulary. In a sense, capillaroscopy satisfies the patient and the reader. The events in the story call into question the material reality of medical practice—the accuracy of diagnosis and the motives of practitioners—while, at the same time, the story itself (because it is a short story) foregrounds its own fictiveness. It brings into sharp relief the issue of authority and the efficacy of words uttered in specific situations—the examining room or a literary narrative.

"Jean Beicke," another early story, is a remarkable portrait as case history. Where "Mind and Body" depicts scientific medicine at an impasse (though psychological power triumphs), "Jean Beicke" shows out-and-out medical failure. The story is a doctor's confession to the reader and an apology for incompetence. In a sense Williams follows Sir William Osler's directions regarding personal integrity and professional honesty. In his 1905 valedictory address to the students at McGill, Osler prescribes the following behavior for the future physician: "Begin early to make a three-fold category—clear cases, doubtful cases, mistakes. And learn to play the game fair, no self-deception, no shrinking from the truth; mercy and consideration for the other man, but none for yourself, upon whom you have to keep an incessant watch."[15] Osler demands a rigorous honesty, which Williams delivers not simply to himself but to anyone who would read the story.

The narrator of "Jean Beicke" is brash and colloquial; rather than reserve, he shows curiosity, anger, happiness, and remorse. The scene is proleptic. Conditions account for the failure: too many babies, not enough nurses, poor sanitation, and birth defects. The doctor's gruff compassion is highlighted by his description of Jean: "I went in when she was just lying there gasping. Somehow or other, I hated to see that kid go. Everybody felt rotten. She was such a scrawny, misshapen, worthless piece of humanity that I had said many times that somebody ought to chuck her in the garbage chute—but after a month of watching her suck up her milk and thrive on it—and to see those alert blue eyes in that face—well, it wasn't pleasant" (*FD* 163). Nevertheless, as the "Ear Man" said, the narrator's diagnosis was "a clear miss." The doctor fails, the patient dies, yet the reader comes away not just with a sense of pathos or tragedy but also with an appreciation of the difficulty involved in practicing medicine: the types of patients treated, economic conditions (the Great Depression), overcrowded hospitals, parental consent (the mother was unavailable when the doctor first wanted to excise the ears), and the problems associated with having genuine compassion and attachment for under-privileged patients. In the face of such overwhelming difficulties, the narrator's bravado rings false. His humor about human garbage becomes macabre—a brittle protective shell hiding a compassionate and sometimes heartbroken human. The peculiar closing line about voting the Communist ticket, rather than actively political, is an expression of helplessness at a hopeless situation.[16] The doctor's confession exerts an inverted power. The profession comes out as fallible but still fighting a valiant effort against overwhelming odds.

It seems peculiar that a profession can gain authority by admitting fallibility, yet in order to convince one must be perceived as not only superior but also honest—a difficult position to hold given the general inaccessibility of medical knowledge. To maintain the authority granted science in Western culture, medicine can be complicated but must also be imbued with a spirit of openness and free inquiry. Thomas Bond, a colonial physician, emphasizes that point in *The Utility of Clinical Lectures* (1766):

> There the Clinical professor comes in to the Aid of Speculation and demonstrates the Truth of Theory by Facts. . . . he meets his pupils at stated times in the Hospital, and when a case presents adapted to his purpose, he asks all those Questions which lead to a certain knowledge of the Disease and parts Affected; and if the Disease baffles the power of Art and the Patient falls a Sacrifice to it, he then brings his Knowledge to the Test, and fixes Honour or discredit on his Reputation by exposing all the Morbid parts to View, and Demonstrates by what means it produced Death, and if perchance he finds something unexpected, which Betrays an Error in Judgement, he like a great and good man immediately acknowledges the mistake, and, for the benefit of survivors, points out other methods by which it might have been more happily treated.[17]

Honesty is part of the professional code, and a doctor—such as the narrator of "Jean Beicke"—who admits a mistake becomes a "great and good man." Bond adds a pragmatic twist to the formula. The mistake furthers the broader cause of medicine by making the doctor sufficiently humble and unlikely to repeat the error, which benefits survivors and, at the same time, provides a corpse that may answer the riddle of a specific malady.

Benjamin Rush, one of the founding fathers of Williams's alma mater, addresses the issue of candor with unusual candor, also showing considerable concern for the reaction of the public: "They [physicians] have often discovered the most extraordinary instances of candour, in acknowledging mistakes of both opinion and practice. Hippocrates has left a testimony against himself, of the loss of a patient, from his inability to distinguish between a suture, and a fracture of the skull; and Dr. Sydenham tells, that he generally lost several of the first patients whom he visited in a new epidemic. This candour is the more meritorious in physicians, as it seldom fails to lessen their credit with the world."[18] Ironically, the doctor is respected both for his skill and (through honesty) his lack of skill.

The relationship of these assertions to "Jean Beicke" and "Mind and Body" (as well as to numerous other texts by Williams) shows a clear irony in the practice of medicine. Practitioners have access to knowledge and technology denied the average citizen and consequently command respect in the community. That respect enables them to practice in the scientifically gray areas explored in "Mind and Body"—a point where the authority of the physician and his use of rhetoric counts for more than his medical skills. Yet from a nearly opposite perspective, physicians can also gain authority through the honesty and openness associated with scientific inquiry. Here one must note that scientific "openness" is, to a great extent, another form of rhetoric that professes free inquiry but in practice regulates rigorously the projects chosen for analysis and the people allowed to enter the laboratory (an issue explored in chapters 2 and 3).

Williams's work further complicates these issues because he moves his exposition of authority and honesty out of the bedside or the hospital to the world of literature. He represents those scenes in fiction and poetry and represents himself as a doctor/poet. Consequently, his honesty and intimidation of patients is laid out before his readers, who judge literary works and actions with different criteria. Many of his stories in which the doctor-patient scene is not clearly present work in ways nonetheless similar to "Mind and Body and "Jean Beicke." Often a storyteller, obviously not Williams, confesses to an event or tells a curiosity. The scene implies Williams as listener and transcriber. The narrators talk through their problems, and Williams, in his role as physician, is the passive listener whose authoritative presence is enough to effect "cure." Readers are then curiously displaced. They hear the same tale told apparently by its original teller, yet are not in Williams's privileged position. In a sense, the reader overhears the tale.

Perhaps most typical of this is "The Knife of the Times," the story of a developing lesbian attachment that has as its climax a sexual confrontation in a pay toilet at Penn Station. "The Knife of the Times" is a long question—a history of affection and a confession of ambiguous urges. In a sense, it is not directed toward the general reader, but rather toward a specific person, the doctor as an authority figure. Because of his education, medical expertise, and a sensitivity that inspires confidence (the essence of bedside manner), the doctor is in a position to offer advice, if not absolution. In his 1910 report to the Carnegie Institute, Abraham Flexner describes what he feels should be the role of the physician in

America: "Upon him society relies to ascertain, and through measures essentially educational to enforce, the conditions that prevent disease and make positively for physical and moral well-being."[19] According to Flexner, the role of the physician is not simply biological but also a function of society. Physicians should coerce proper moral behavior from their patients.

Gilbert Sorrentino has demonstrated the speaker's multiple voices in his essay "Polish Mothers and 'The Knife of the Times,'" noting that the narrator is not omniscient but closer to absent first person.[20] Maura is that absent first person, at least up to the last line, which, like many of Williams's final lines, is ambiguous: "Why not?" (*FD* 6). It can be read at least two different ways: Maura has confessed the story to her physician, Dr. Williams, and is asking his opinion of her reciprocating Ethel's affections. Another possibility is that Williams the author is asking the reader for a response. Given the second, the story now cuts in two directions. Maura confesses her plight to the doctor, who presumably listens and gives advice. He then confesses the story to the reader and asks the same question. As a physician, Williams is in a position to elicit, indeed command, such a confession from his patient, who is genuinely troubled by her situation. As an author, he can present the case as something of an oddity, as a touch of the scandal that a doctor must encounter almost daily, and he can further scandalize the reader by asking the question, why not? Given Flexner's definition of the physician and the medical profession's long history of moral management, one would expect censure of a lesbian affair (or at least a medical explanation of its "unnaturalness") instead of a jocular wink of the eye. Although the doctor is virtually absent from the narration, the scene is reminiscent of many "doctor stories." Williams, as a physician, has been privy to this "scandalous" story and can further scandalize his readers both with the story and his own tolerance.

As "The Knife of the Times" shows, many of Williams's short stories place the reader in an odd position in relation to literary and medical authority. He or she becomes a voyeur, eavesdropping on supposedly privileged conversations between a doctor and his patients. As a physician, Williams is privy to the material, but the reader can only look on from a point far to the outside. In "The Physician and Authority" Suzanne Poirier discusses several physicians, Williams among them, noting that the novelist and physician S. Weir Mitchell relished the medical authority granted to him by society, while "Williams does not glorify his profession or his power."[21] The doctor in Williams's stories, though brash at times, is more often humble. Williams's own medical authority is often undercut in the various dramatic scenes he creates, but the undercutting paradoxically creates more authority. Compared to Weir Mitchell and the way he textually presents himself treating patients, Williams certainly does not glory in his power; nonetheless, he is quite adept at using it in ways not easily detected.[22] The (often ill-defined) medical setting for many of Williams's texts, while it carries with it the cultural authority of the physician practicing in America, is complicated by the literary enframing, which creates different relations to authority and honesty.

One of Williams's most complex treatments of the doctor's relationship with his patients and his social milieu is "Old Doc Rivers." It is a remarkable story because of its subject—the emergence of modern suburban medicine—and its narrative form, which is perhaps the most sophisticated in Williams's fiction. The peculiar mixture of idolatry and disgust, reflected in the alternating narrators and anecdotes, shows Williams and the society in which he finds himself coming to grips with the charismatic power of medical authority.[23] Similar to "Jean Beicke" and, to a lesser extent, "Mind and Body," "Old Doc Rivers" is a hymn to the medical establishment. In a complex and ambiguous way, Williams succeeds in elevating at least one practitioner to medical sainthood.

Using bits of the history of American medicine, Williams shows Rivers to be the last of the snake oil quacks and, at the same time, the prototype of the modern suburban physician. The story's focus on transportation traces the historical movement that, perhaps more than any other, transformed medical practice. In *The Social Transformation of American Medicine* Paul Starr argues that improved transportation, almost more than any other change, helped the emergence of the modern medical profession because it enabled more doctors to see more patients in less time.[24] It also allowed both doctors and patients to travel greater distances, thus opening up the possibility of competition and consultation. And finally, it opened the suburbs. The countryside was transformed into communities of wealthy commuters and poor factory workers. As a result, the medical profession's very structure, its way of doing business, was radically altered. Doc Rivers can be seen at the vanguard of this transformation, operating a large, sprawling practice and even having one of the first telephones. From another perspective, he is still a simple country doctor who loves to hunt and fish, helps anyone in need, operates on his patients' kitchen tables, does not specialize, and, most important, has no book-keeping ledgers, specific office hours (except Sundays), or anything that even smells like American efficiency. He is what many nostalgically view as a professional, which is just to say that he was superior to commercialism.

Williams's own sense of medicine in transition is reflected in several narrative intrusions on the commodification of medical practice. In the first comment, meant in part to justify Rivers's as-yet-unnamed problem, Williams's narrator says, "It was not money. It came of his sensitivity, his civility; it was that that made him do it, I'm sure; the antithesis rather of that hog-like complacency that comes to so many men following the successful scamper for cash" (*FD* 82). As doctors began to make more and more money, their altruistic motives became increasingly suspect. That change is perhaps most evident in the narrator's defense of Rivers: "Naturally, he must have given value for value, good services for money received. He had a record of thirty years behind him, finally, for getting there (provided you could find him) anywhere, anytime, for anybody—no distinctions; and for doing something, mostly the right thing, without delay and of his own initiative, once he was there" (*FD* 79). Here medicine is a commodity pure and simple, and its value outside the economic is its democratic impulse, "anywhere, anytime, for anybody." The narrator's frequent assertion that "money was never an end with him" (*FD* 87) reflects a profession trying to hold onto an abstract ideal but finally being forced into monetary measurement. This is the heart of "Old Doc Rivers" as it relates to medicine. If the institution provides something more than health in exchange for money, its agents must somehow be remarkable.

As one would suspect, however, this medical hero has a tragic flaw—dope addiction.[25] In Williams's construction, it is the result of the compassion felt by this otherwise extraordinary human for the poor and the wretched around him. In this way, Williams can alternate positive and negative anecdotes, with the positive demonstrating Rivers's uncanny ability as diagnostician and the negative reflecting not his personal failings but rather the flawed world in which they occur. Rivers is a strong, sensitive man, "a man trying to fill his place among those lacking the power to grasp his innate capabilities" (*FD* 90). He was a remarkable diagnostician in part because he studied pathology in Freiburg.[26] The bulk of his patients were "a population in despair, out of hand, out of discipline, driven about by each other blindly, believing in the miraculous, the drunken, as it may be. Here was, to many, though they are diminishing fast, something before which they could worship, a local shrine, all there was left, a measure of the poverty which surrounded them" (*FD* 104).

Nevertheless, "Old Doc Rivers" is critical of the medical establishment, particularly the conspiracy of silence promoted by the AMA.[27] Williams's narrator is bitter over the possibility of professional misconduct:

> My wife would sometimes say to me, If you know he is killing people, why do you doctors not get together and have his license taken away from him?
> I would answer that I didn't know. I doubted that we could prove anything. No one wanted to try. (*FD* 103)

Yet the story serves to canonize precisely the most guilty. Lured by the charismatic image of the doctor, Williams's narrator, like the poor and superstitious laborers, succumbs to the power of medical authority. He is obsessed with discovering "What kind of a doctor was he, really?" (*FD* 80). His impulse, similar to that of *In the American Grain,* is to discover at the root what makes this practitioner (or any person) remarkable. His strategy is also similar to that of his book of American history in that the narrator goes back to the written record to attempt to reconstruct the basis for his charismatic doctor, those "heavy ledgers, serious and interesting in appearance with their worn leather covers and gold lettering across the front" (*FD* 80). He succeeds through these texts and numerous eyewitness accounts to construct a picture of a man who practiced a medicine that depended not simply on scientific skill but also on "mystery, necromancy, cures—charms of all sorts" (*FD* 101). The story ends with Rivers triumphant—set up downtown across from the municipal building like a monument. The story itself is something of a monument in the Williams canon. It is his longest sustained impression of the charismatic power of his profession.

"Old Doc Rivers" shows the charismatic authority of the medical profession jostling against its pretensions toward being a science. A truly scientific medicine would have no need for the Doc Rivers of the world. All diagnosis and treatment would be part of an objective decision based on clear conceptual categories and data from standardized inscription devices. But medicine had not (and has not) achieved that status and consequently depends on authority stemming from both its science and its art (categories that do not hold up well on inspection, as "Old Doc Rivers" demonstrates). One of the most important advocates of scientific medicine was Claude Bernard, whose *Introduction to the Study of Experimental Medicine* (1865) deals obliquely with the issue:

> The progress of the experimental method consists in this,—that the sum of truths grows larger in proportion as the sum of error grows less. But each one of these particular truths is added to the rest to establish more general truths. In this fusion, the names of promoters of science disappear little by little, and the further science advances, the more it takes an impersonal form and detaches itself from the past. To avoid a mistake which has sometimes been committed, I hasten to add that I mean to speak here of the evolution of science only. In arts and letters, personality dominates everything.[28]

Bernard is clearly at pains to distinguish the true path of medicine from its dominance by charismatic practitioners, relegating their power to the ineffectual realm of art.[29] Bernard's text is a plea to throw off the yoke of tradition, but he still recognizes the reliance of medical practice on charisma: "We see [medicine] still more or less mingled with religion and with the supernatural. Superstition and the marvelous play a great part in it. Sorcerers, somnambulists, healers by virtue of some gift from Heaven, are held as the equals of physicians. Medical personality is placed above science by physicians themselves; they seek their authority in tradition, in doctrines or in medical tact. This state of affairs is clearest of proofs that the experimental method has by no means come into its own in medicine."[30] The same state of affairs is what makes "Old Doc Rivers" an important historical text. Williams is positioned as part of the first generation of American doctors fully trained in scientific medicine, and his young narrator is looking back at a physician who practiced through the shift and thus participated in both worlds. Williams can hold up Rivers as a relic of a bygone medical era, but he cannot shake off the power of the charismatic healer. The authority of the medical profession remains, regardless of Bernard's pleas, intimately tied with the residues of religion, superstition, and faith healing, and doctors continue to be concerned about their tenuously held social authority. "Old Doc Rivers" is also significant in Williams's canon as it charts the emergence of modernism, which is a movement striving for objectivity yet also tied to the residues of religion and superstition and obsessed with the authority of the author.[31]

CHAPTER 2

Against Theory: The Rhetoric of Clarity

It would be difficult to point out any observer who excels him in devotion to truth, and freedom from the trammels of theory or prejudice. He tells plainly what he saw and leaves everyone to draw his own inferences, or where he lays down conclusions he does so with a degree of modesty and fairness of which few perhaps in his circumstances would have been capable.
—*Andrew Combe praising William Beaumont*

All sciences and philosophies, all the various categories of intellectual investigation and in metaphysics. Art alone remains always concrete, objective.
—The Embodiment of Knowledge

The objects in nature and the results of calculation are clearly and cleanly formed; they are organized without ambiguity. It is because we see clearly *that we can read, learn and feel their harmony. I repeat:* clear statement *is essential in a work of art.*
—*Le Corbusier*

Williams's epistemology is defined in the *Embodiment of Knowledge:* "Clarity is the word. That is the power of it, as a whole—not the humanity, not the this, the that, but as a whole it stands outside and—is clear. A clean wind through the chaff of truth. Alive again: This is what throws off poetry. Direct vision—knowledge to action, to knowledge: Clarity is rare" (*EK* 33–34). Nearly all his statements regarding the purpose of poetry and the attainment of knowledge return to the direct apprehension of a clear, unadorned object. First and foremost a poet must be able to see and detail in living language the fragments of everyday life—broken bottles, tethered goats, or Queen Anne's lace.

From a literary standpoint, Williams's desire for clear vision and articulation can best be traced to the early influence of Ezra Pound, whose famous rules for Imagism include "Direct treatment of the 'thing' whether subjective or objective," and "To use absolutely no word that does not contribute to the presentation."[1] With these rules Pound raises related but separate problems. The first demands the ability to see and know the "thing" as thing, and the second requires a language capable of re-presenting that thing clearly. He goes on to admire Daniel and Cavalcanti in much the same terms: "I have seen that precision which I miss in the Victorians, that explicit rendering, be it of external nature, or of emotion. Their testimony is of the eyewitness, their symptoms are first hand."[2] The legalistic (as well as medical) overtones of this comment bring together the two rules: not only must eyewitnesses be able to articulate accurately what they have seen, but they must also be credible. Their testimony must seem objective in order to convince; consequently, the notion of being an eyewitness is part of a rhetoric of clarity.

Later Williams became associated with Objectivism, a movement defined by Louis Zukofsky: "An Objective: (Optics)—the lens bringing the rays from an object to a focus. That which is aimed at. . . . Desire for what is objectively perfect, inextricably the direction of historic and contemporary particulars."[3] Zukofsky's use of optics (the science of the gaze) and "desire" in the same formula is a crucial pairing. By showing that the gaze is anything but passive, the Objectivists set out to counter the simple registering of visual detail by some of the later imagists. In his definition of *Objectivism* for the Princeton *Encyclopedia of Poetry and Poetics,* Williams emphasizes an active gaze: "The mind rather than the unsupported eye entered the picture." Although they were primarily concerned with the poem as an object in itself, the Objectivists never lost sight of the problems associated with the objective rendering of facts. An "unsupported" eye (Emerson's "transparent eyeball") might be the ideal for objective observation, but biologically and philosophically it was impossible.

Zukofsky ends his preface to An *"Objectivists" Anthology* with the following: "The mind may construct its world—this is hardly philosophy—if the mind does construct its world there is always that world immanent or imminently outside which at least as a term has become an entity."[4] With this statement Zukofsky dismisses phenomenological problems, and most of the time, Williams joins him in that attitude. Nevertheless, Williams's medical education showed him how the senses are trained to perceive that world "imminently outside," and thus how the mind shapes it. Williams's minute codification of specific detail is not simply a new way to write poetry. It is also an attempt to deal with the epistemological problems of diagnosis. He presses the double question Pound's rules imply: what details are significant and how can they be read and represented clearly and with conviction?

In his report to the Carnegie Foundation, Abraham Flexner writes, "I have argued that . . . medicine has accepted the fundamental criterion of science, for it is pledged to the critical scrutiny of facts, as far as our powers aided by every known device can carry us."[5] For Flexner, truth is made of "facts," which are objects capable of being observed by an "objective" eye with the technology of the age. In remarkably similar terms, A. C. Abbott (Williams's instructor and author of the bacteriology textbook he used at the University of Pennsylvania) discusses Antonj van Leeuwenhoek: "[His] paper [presented to the Royal Society of London in 1683] is of particular importance, not only because of the careful, objective nature of the description given of the bodies seen by him, but also for the illustrations which accompany it. From a perusal of the text and an inspection of the plates there remains little doubt that Leeuwenhoek saw with his primitive lens the bodies now recognized as bacteria. . . . Throughout all of Leeuwenhoek's work there is a conspicuous absence of the speculative. His contributions are remarkable for their purely objective nature."[6] Abbott's praise for Leeuwenhoek depends on a rhetoric that values clearly represented details, particularly if those representations are accurate according to modern standards, and have been accomplished with a "primitive" technology. Abbott's Leeuwenhoek deserves further praise for avoiding ambiguous language through his illustrations, an important element in the rhetoric of clarity. Objectivity for Flexner, Abbott, Pound, and Zukofsky depends on visual perception and subsequent representation: the ability to pierce through obscurity to see and say the thing clearly.

Between 1928 and 1930 Williams pieced together the notes on educational reform that would be later published as *The Embodiment of Knowledge*. The overriding metaphor of that text is a medical anecdote: "Children, at birth, used to be made blind by a venereal infection of the eyes, until we used silver nitrate in every case" (*EK* 26). For Williams, who as a pediatrician witnessed countless deliveries, birth is a fresh beginning—a time of clear perceptions. *The Embodiment of Knowledge* is directed specifically against a society that raises its children with an unenlightened educative system, and Williams's own stab at educational reform is articulated in terms of the eye. People do not think clearly because they do not see clearly. When encumbered by philosophy or theoretical science, the mind cannot grasp the object (a tree or a poem) as object. Williams's crusade in *The Embodiment of Knowledge* and his poetic crusade (embodied in the poems) is to throw off what restricts vision—the congenital blindness of tradition—so that objective and poetic truth can be revealed in its naked splendor.

In his introduction to *Medicine and Literature,* Edmund D. Pellegrino notes the affinities between the practice of medicine and the practice of poetry: "For both are ways of looking at man and both are, at heart, moral enterprises. Both must start by seeing life bare, without averting their gaze."[7] Pellegrino's emphasis on the "gaze" and seeing "life bare" is telling. Williams's poetic sensibility is permeated by a clinical sensibility: in essence, much of his writing is what Marie Boroff calls a practice of the "diagnostic eye."[8] Williams's epistemology demands the exploration of the fetters to the clear apprehension of truth or objective clarity, and consequently it roots him in a deep historical tradition of medicine—the dialectical play between direct apprehension of the thing and the broader enframing of that data in a rational or theoretical field. Fleck notes: "Simple lack of 'direct contact with nature' during experimental dissection cannot explain the frequency of the phrase 'which becomes visible during autopsy' often accompanying what to us seem the most absurd assertions."[9] He goes on to argue that "Cognition is the most socially conditioned activity of man, and knowledge is the paramount social creation [*Gebilde*]."[10] *The Embodiment of Knowledge* explores in its own uncertain way how to achieve clear vision and reveals Williams's ambivalence about the pretensions of science and the possibilities of any firm knowledge.

In *The Evolution of Modern Medicine* Sir William Osler characterizes his sense of the history of medicine as the progressive abandonment of restrictive theories in favor of clearly observable data. According to Osler, the importance of minute cataloguing of objective detail was established by Hippocrates at the beginning of Western medicine: "A keen observer and an active practitioner, his views of disease thus hastily sketched, dominated the profession for twenty five centuries; indeed, echoes of his theories are still heard in the schools, and his very words are daily on our lips. If asked what was the great contribution to medicine of Hippocrates and his school we could answer—the art of careful observation."[11] Avicenna (980–1037) saved the Hippocratic and Galenic texts after the fall of Rome, and his *Canon medicinae* became the standard Medieval medical text. The spirit of inquisitiveness expressed by both Hippocrates and Galen was lost in the transfer, however. The Avicennian texts were long considered definitive and unquestionable.[12] Centuries would pass before that hegemony would begin to crumble (Paracelsus burned the *Canon* publicly), but the terms of the fight remain. Practitioners retain allegiance to the abstract models of medicine (the great texts) in which they were trained, and reformers reject them on the basis of divergent empirical evidence.

The fight against medical dogmatism depicted by Osler is epitomized in Vesalius's *De humani corporis fabrica* (1543). Vesalius laments the abstraction of medicine, arguing that, since the invasions of the Goths, physicians had lost their curiosity. They no longer used their hands but instead memorized the sacred texts and instructed their servants to do the actual work. Reversing that trend, he became one of medicine's great anatomists, dissecting numerous corpses himself and setting down his findings in minute detail. An argument from one of his public dissections characterizes the debate between advocates of clear presentation and those of traditional erudition:

When the lecture of Curtius was finished, Vesalius, who had been present and heard the refutation of his arguments, asked Curtius to accompany him to the anatomy. For he wanted to show him that his theory was quite true. . . . Now, he said . . . here we have our bodies. We shall see whether I have made an error. Now we want to look at this and we should in the meantime leave Galen, for I acknowledge that I have said, if it is permissible to say so, that here Galen is in the wrong, because he did not know the position of the vein without pair in the human body, which is the same to-day as it was in his time. Curtius answered smiling, for Vesalius, choleric as he was, was very excited: No, he said, Domine, we must not leave Galen, because he always well understood everything, and, consequently, we also follow him. Do you know how to interpret Hippocrates better than Galen did? Vesalius answered: I do not say so, but I show you here in these bodies the vein without pair, [and] how it nourishes all the lower ribs.[13]

Curtius wants to respect what is written in the sacred texts, and Vesalius prefers to read the body, which, ideally, produces a truth all may come to see. Here is Williams's professional heritage and poetic ideal. As he puts it, "Doctrinaire formula-worship—that is our real enemy" (*I* 279). Rejecting dogmatism and tradition, the doctor and the poet must examine objects up close—smell, taste, touch—and detail them in language in order to create a diagnosis or poem that is knowledge, clarity, and action.

The desire to see the object clearly is fraught with difficulty, however. The history of medicine (particularly anatomy) is pervaded by what today would be considered blatant misreadings based on culturally constituted ways of seeing. Vesalius's own texts contain many such constructions. For example, his depiction of the uterus and vagina, following the thought of his day, bears remarkable similarity to the male sexual organs (see figure 1). His debate with Curtius raises clearly an ongoing problem in medical education and practice: there is a need for hands-on examination of patients and charting of symptoms, but medical science must also create abstract models of pathology. Unfortunately, those abstractions can become fossilized metaphors restricting the clear vision Williams prizes.

As technology changed, the privileging of the senses over abstraction and erudition increased. That shift is perhaps best demonstrated by the invention of the microscope, the stethoscope, and chest percussion. Marcello Malpighi (1628–94) and Antonj van Leeuwenhoek (1632–1723) each independently used the newly invented microscope to study the movement of the blood, discovering capillaries in the process. Their discovery is important because it clears up arguments about circulation, directly attacks the four-humors theory (and most canonical medicine), and does so through the use of the eye. Leeuwenhoek's discussion of his discovery of capillaries makes a familiar appeal: "If now we see clearly with our eyes that the passing of the blood from the arteries into the veins, in the tadpoles, only takes place in such blood-vessels as are so thin that only one corpuscle can be driven through at one time, we may conclude that the same thing takes place in the same way in our bodies as well as in that of all animals."[14] That simple

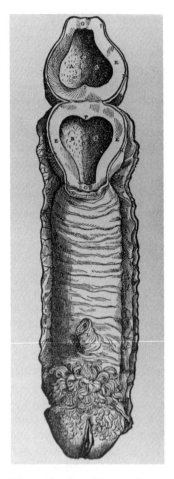

Fig. 1. Vesalius, "Uterus, Vagina and External Pudenda," *Anatomical Drawings of Vesalius,* 1543.

assertion carries tremendous rhetorical weight. It is conditional (not all might be able to see), but those privileged with clear sight may become good scientists and doctors. The sentence construction assures its assent proleptically: what is true is what is seen by those gifted with "sight." Leeuwenhoek's appeal to a rhetoric of clarity is a remarkably effective strategy, since seeing *is* believing— Vesalius vanquishes Curtius.

Slowly empiricism gained ground over canonical medicine. Leopold Auenbrugger's use of percussion (1761) replaced theoretical speculation with an objective "value-free" method: "What I have written I have proved again and again, by the testimony of my own senses, and amid laborious and tedious exertions;—still guarding, on all occasions, against the seductive influence of self-love."[15] Auenbrugger's "sounds" were (and to some extent still are) notoriously difficult to reproduce and interpret, however. It took years of refinement before any sense of continuity or aural standardization was developed. In other words, the senses must be trained. Along with Auenbrugger's percussion is René Laënnec's invention of the stethoscope, which resulted not from a methodological problem (how to hear the heartbeat of an obese, large-breasted woman) but rather from moral squeamishness: "The patient's age and sex did not permit me to resort to the kind of examination I have just described (i.e., direct application of the ear to the chest)."[16] Regardless of its origin, the stethoscope provides for amplification of the senses in relation to the actual physical body, further privileging empiricism in the practice of medicine.

That empiricism came into its own in the middle nineteenth century with the rise of the clinical method, led by the French physicians Pierre Cabanis and Philippe Pinel and promulgated to many important American practitioners by Pierre Louis (e.g., Oliver Wendell Holmes, G. C. Shattuck, James Jackson, Jr., and Henry Bowditch). Pinel argued vigorously for simplifying the pharmacopeia and teaching medicine at the bedside rather than from books: "[The clinical method] is the best method to train the students' judgement rather than their memory, and to focus their attention on perceivable evidence."[17] The clinical method depended on the careful display of clear cases, and consequently caused the doctors to focus on specific symptoms, at times to the detriment of their patient's general well-being: "It is obvious that medical observations can be precise and conclusive only if the evidence is reduced to the smallest possible number of facts and to the plainest data."[18] In America, clinical medicine's emphasis on empirical observation paved the way for some of the midcentury educational reforms. Theoretical medicine, represented by miracle cure-alls or holistic concepts of health, was derided in favor of carefully detailed sensory observations. John Harley Warner notes that "the methodological meaning of *empirical* became steadily more positive as physicians deliberately turned to clinical experience and questioning of theory as a way to reform medical knowledge."[19]

The clinical epistemology also lay the groundwork for the rise of laboratory medicine. Clinical medicine depends on the isolation of patients in wards, separate from their personal surroundings and, after hospital reform, in nearly a different climate. The French insistence on close observation of specific symptoms as they arose in patients created tremendous diagnostic breakthroughs. The laboratory's isolation of specific germs and bacteria is, in a sense, the logical extension of the rhetoric of clarity. But laboratory medicine, fueled by the spectacular successes of Pasteur, Lister, and Koch as well as the public health work of men such of Walter Reed, moved well beyond the passivity of clinical medicine. In 1858 Rudolf Virchow published his monumental *Cellular Pathology* and launched his own antitraditional attack: "We declared war on formulas and demanded positive experience, to be gained to the greatest possible extent in an empirical manner with the aid of, and in the light of, the tools available. We asked for the emancipation of pathology and therapy from the oppression of the ancillary sciences, and we recognized as the sole means to this end the rejection of all medical systems, the destruction of medical sects, and the fight against medical dogmatism."[20]

Claude Bernard's *Introduction to the Study of Experimental Medicine* is one of the primary texts of the laboratory revolution. Rather than supporting Pinel, Louis, and Cabanis, Bernard advocates a therapeutic position to fill the void left by the midcentury skeptics, that is, to move the power of medicine and therapeutics to the lab.[21] German laboratory methods, typified by Koch, were important for this shift to what John Harley Warner calls the "New Rationalism"—a turn away from France to a "scientific" (experimental) medicine. Yet even in the midst of his articles of faith, Bernard shows some skepticism (a skepticism that permeates much of the science/art discussion about medicine even today): "we must believe in science, i.e., in determinism; we must believe in a complete and necessary relation between things, among the phenomena proper to living beings as well as in all others; but at the same time we must be thoroughly convinced that we know this relation only in a more or less approximate way, and that the theories we hold are far from embodying changeless truths."[22] Bernard sets up the possibility of a scientifically decodable nature, but maintains a degree of humility in the face of the project. His humility contains elements of the same antitheoretical position that runs through much of medical history. Nevertheless, his remedy is a rigorous laboratory method: "The great experimental principle, then, is doubt, that philosophic doubt which leaves to the mind its freedom and initiative, and from which the virtues most valuable to investigators in physiology and medicine are derived. We must trust our observations or our theories only after experimental verification. If we trust too much, the mind becomes bound and cramped by the results of its own reasoning; it no longer has freedom of action, and so lacks the power to break away from that blind faith in theories which is only scientific superstition."[23]

In the United States, the founding of Johns Hopkins Medical School marked the ascendancy of scientific medicine. William Welch addressed the medical school on several important occasions, and in doing so, he set down the principles of what was to become medical education in America. In 1893 he invoked the antitheoretical model in language, which echoes the Emersonian tradition: "The Johns Hopkins Medical School will start unhampered by traditions and free to work out its own salvation."[24] Johns Hopkins's teaching would be based in part on the French school. The students would learn on the wards: "The aim of the school is primarily to train practitioners well grounded in the fundamental medical sciences and in practical medicine and surgery and their branches. We have broken completely with the old idea that reading books and listening to lectures is an adequate training for those who are to assume the responsible duties of practitioners of medicine."[25] But Welch's method is qualified considerably in admissions requirements, curriculum, and attitude. Hopkins was the first medical school to require a bachelor's degree and rigorous undergraduate training in the basic sciences. The scientific background adds to the simple knowledge gained through clinical training: "The advantages of thus coming throughout the entire course into direct personal contact with the objects of study are not merely that the students thereby acquire a more useful and living knowledge of them, but that they become familiar with scientific methods and acquire something of the scientific spirit of investigation and of approaching medical problems."[26] New American doctors were now going to be first and foremost scientists. That scientific bent was exemplified at the University of Pennsylvania Medical School by the construction of the Medical Laboratories Building at the turn of the century. Education now took place not just in the Medical Building (now Logan Hall) and the hospital, but also in the labyrinthine laboratories where the truth of disease is understood, not through the body of the patient lying sick in his or her own home, but instead through the examination of that patient's cells on a microscope slide.[27]

The history of modern medicine can be seen as the systematic rejection of abstraction. Its impulse is antitheoretical; its ideal is praxis. Flexner summarizes the antitheoretical position in terms remarkably similar to Williams's own statements of poetics:

The modern point of view may be restated as follows: medicine is a discipline, in which the effort is made to use knowledge procured in various ways in order to effect certain practical ends. With abstract general propositions it has nothing to do. It harbors no preconceptions as to diseases or their cure. Instead of starting with a finished and supposedly adequate dogma or principle, it has progressively become less cocksure and more modest. It distrusts general propositions, *a priori* explanations, grandiose and comforting generalizations. It needs theories only as convenient summaries in which a number of ascertained facts may be used tentatively to define a course of action. It makes no effort to use its discoveries to substantiate a principle formulated before the facts were even suspected. For it has learned from the previous history of human thought that men possessed of vague preconceived ideas are strongly disposed to force facts to fit, defend, or explain them. And this tendency both interferes with the free search for truth and limits the good which can be extracted from such truth as is in its despite attained.[28]

Flexner clearly finds himself within the American pragmatist tradition—one that emphasizes the direct perception of the object in its local circumstances and resists movement toward the universal except as it is sanctioned by those circumstances.

Williams reflects that attitude in his writing. In *The Embodiment of Knowledge,* which celebrates adolescence because it is presystematic, he calls Shakespeare his grandfather because he is "free . . . of theory" (*EK* 112). The disdain held by reformers in the medical profession for dogmatic thought is clearly represented in "The Descent of Winter":

> He would go
> out to pick herbs, he graduate of
> the old university. He would go out
> and ask that old woman, in the little
> village by the lake, to show him wild
> ginger. He himself would not know the plant.
> (*I* 251)

In one sense, this poem is an attack on Eliot and Pound—those of the old university who would not know "life" if they saw it but instead live it secondhand through texts. Compared to them, Williams is the old woman who can show them real plants. In another sense Williams is the one who is educated (in the manner he attacks in *The Embodiment of Knowledge*), and he must rely on his patients to provide life, to show him flowers or cure with flaxseed poultices. From that perspective, the educated person, just like anatomists before Vesalius, is a voyeur. In order to gain knowledge, he or she must cast off preconceived notions of truth and follow the woman to the lake.

The problems inherent in imagism and objectivism are paralleled in medicine. If empirical evidence is privileged over abstraction (theory, rationality, tradition), then one must have eyes unclouded by Francis Bacon's "Idols." In addition, this clear vision must be articulated. In medicine that articulation results in a remarkably opaque discourse guaranteed communicative by years of user indoctrination. Ideally, medical education trains the senses and at the same time secures its discourse from ambiguity. Conversely, in much modern poetry, language is regarded with suspicion. Meaning is slippery and can only be provisionally guaranteed through the economy of the plain style (interestingly, a style whose primary contours resemble those dictated by the rules of the Royal Society). Williams's familiar insistence on the "American idiom" can be seen as a way of assuring (democratically) the clearest and broadest possible communication. (This issue is examined more closely in chapters 3 and 4.)

In his texts, these problems—clear sight and articulation—are foregrounded; consequently, understanding his sense of the meaning of the term *science* is crucial. His numerous statements regarding science seem overly dismissive and, at times, incoherent.[29] By approaching his discussions of it through the lens of the medical history just recounted, however, they become clearer. Although he often made references to science throughout his career (his debt to Charles Steinmetz and Alfred North Whitehead and his ideas about relativity are discussed in chapter 8), Williams confronted the issue of science, art, and society primarily in the texts he produced between *Spring and All* (1923) and *A Novelette and Other Prose* (1932). There the word refers to different practices depending on its immediate context; yet when the comments are taken as a whole, a coherent pattern emerges.

It is not surprising, given the medical tradition, that Williams's most negative sense of science usually refers to the practice of creating abstract categories. Discussing observations of natural phenomena (mercury and water's expansion and contraction relative to temperature change) in *A Novelette,* he observes: "When these things were first noted categories were ready for them so that they got fast in corners of understanding. By this process, reinforced by tradition, every common thing has been nailed down, stripped of freedom of action and taken away from use. This is the origin of trips to the poles, trips of discovery, suicides and the inability to see clearly" (*I* 295–96). Williams is describing what Thomas Kuhn, in *The Structure of Scientific Revolutions,* calls a "paradigm." Although the rigidity of Kuhn's original formulation has been attacked and modified by later social studies of science, his initial definition echoes the complaints lodged by physicians throughout history against established or traditional categories of thought:

> I mean to suggest that some accepted examples of actual scientific practice— examples which include law, theory, application, and instrumentation to-gether—provide models from which spring particular coherent traditions of scientific research. . . . The study of paradigms . . . is what mainly prepares the student for membership in the particular scientific community with which he will later practice. Because he there joins men who learned the bases of their field from the same concrete models, his subsequent practice will sel-dom evoke overt disagreement over fundamentals. Men whose research is based on shared paradigms are committed to the same rules and standards for scientific practice. That commitment and the apparent consensus it produces are prerequisites for normal science, i.e., for the genesis and continuation of a particular research tradition.[30]

Like the poetic tradition, the scientific tradition (institutional indoctrination) carries with it specific methods and practices; con-sequently, it defines clear vision and controls individual freedom of action.[31] Even though the conceptual categories Williams and, implicitly, Kuhn deride are necessary if one is even to focus on an object, Williams tries to maintain a level of freedom for both the objects and the observer outside historically constructed percep-tual categories. He does this by rejecting heavy-handed tradition and recognizing that categories cannot exhaust the meaning or the power of a single object. Instead, the materiality of that object always exceeds an observer's ability to capture it. If science is simply the practice of imposing categories on phenomena, Wil-liams wants nothing to do with it.

As early as *Kora in Hell* he attacks the creation of simple catego-ries by way of resemblance, preferring to remain focused on the specific object at hand: "Although it is a quality of the imagination that it seeks to place together those things which have a common relationship, yet the coining of similes is a pastime of very low order, depending as it does upon a nearly vegetable coincidence. Much more keen is that power which discovers in things those inimitable particles of dissimilarity to all other things which are the peculiar perfections of the thing in question" (*I* 18). Here his training in medicine is set up against the broader pretensions of pure science. In his schema, the normal scientist is concerned with relationships ("the coining of similes"), but the physician confronted with illness is concerned with the pathological—"those inimitable particles of dissimilarity." He goes on in *A Novelette* to criticize the promises science offers society: "Science is impotent from all the viewpoints from which in its inception it seemed to promise enlightenment to the human mind. It is going nowhere but to gross and minute codification of the perceptions" (*I* 305). This version of science cannot provide knowledge. If its paradigm precedes its perceptions, science is part of the tradition of Curtius, shutting itself off from the specifics of observation. Its perceptual and categorical apparatuses dominate, control, and code the unique specificity of the individual object.[32]

This criticism does not show that Williams rejects science, however. Rather, these statements align him with that medical tradition whose business is the rejection of medical tradition. In *The Embodiment of Knowledge* he attacks science as a privileged practice, but at the same time points to what he feels is its true function: "Science be it remembered, changes nothing, invents nothing, takes away nothing, adds nothing to the material world. How can it? It does one thing only—it brings its material into a certain relationship with the intelligence, in its relationship with man and poetry, brings man into a diagonal relationship with it" (*EK* 129). In other words, the goal of science is not enlightenment in and of itself; rather, its promise is to help people (scientists and nonscientists alike) confront the particulars of the world without being blinded by a paralytic tradition. The skepticism of modern science toward abstraction makes more possible the direct apprehension of the thing. By bringing material "into a diagonal relationship" with the observer, it provides a way of seeing that is provisionally freer than other human practices.

From this perspective, science is one of the many ways humans produce knowledge. In words that could have been either Osler or Flexner discussing the situation of modern medicine, Williams describes the relationship of science and philosophy to art: "As they leave superstition behind they (Science and Philosophy, etc.) approach the conditions of art of which, in reality, they are particular departments" (*EK* 92). Art (or knowledge—Williams often conflates the two) is a larger, more inclusive vision because science cannot know its own end. Williams's sense of that vision is detailed in an almost epiphanic moment in *The Embodiment of Knowledge:* "Knowledge itself seemed defined in a new and unmistakable manner. There was a roundness which granted several diameters which could be named science, philosophy, history, literature—all of which must be an aspect of this thing. I felt it and saw it definitely before me. I felt satisfied" (*EK* 76–77). As long as science, philosophy, history and literature are enabling, as long as they are tools for attaining art (which is knowledge), Williams will use them. When they become ends unto themselves, he abandons them.

Williams's ambivalence toward science also shows a fundamental fracture in the medical profession's discourse. Because of the pressure of the past (the heavy hand of Avicennian traditionalism), medicine must guard against abstraction. It must stick close to the specific details of the body. Yet post-Baconian science is nothing without induction. One maintains contact in order to abstract. An autopsy is performed to determine the etiology of a disease because it could strike another body. When a specific disorder or malfunction is named, however, it becomes an abstraction. Medicine establishes itself in large part within the discourse of "science" (the science embodied by the abstract categories Williams rejects), yet its history forces continuous deconstruction of that position. It speaks the scientifically established truth, yet must undercut that truth's efficacy if it tends toward the general. This paradox is, in a large part, a source of Williams's universal in the local dictum, which is not simply polemical but is also a manifestation of a contradiction in medical thought.

Williams's treatment for these problems is his doctrine of "contact." On the surface, the idea is quite simple, yet in the first few issues of *Contact* (a little magazine he edited with Robert McAlmon) (1920) he successfully obscures it with some of his most opaque commentary: "*Contact* . . . [is] issued in the conviction that art which attains is indigenous of experience and relations, and that the artist works to express perceptions rather than to attain standards of achievement: however much information and past art may have served to clarify his perceptions and sophisticate his comprehensions, they will be no standard by which his work shall be adjudged. For if there are standards in reality and in existence if there are values and relations which are absolute, they will apply to art. Otherwise any standard of criticism is a mere mental exercise, and past art signifies nothing" (1). Art that attains the status of "art" is good, according to the *Contact*'s standard, because it expresses local, indigenous perceptions. Williams recognizes that past art and information (traditional perceptual frames) exert influence, but they are not the criteria for judgment. The brilliance (albeit accidental) of the sentence "For if there are standards . . ." is that its very obscurity makes the existence of the essences to which it refers ambiguous. This manifesto echoes a grammatical pattern Williams often used: there is no way to place the prepositional phrase "in existence," given the context of the sentence. It floats, shimmering like the mirage of objective truth, in the middle of what could be an argument for ideal form or poetic anarchy. The true standard is saved for the opening clause of the next paragraph: "We are here because of our faith in the existence of native artists who are capable of having, comprehending and recording extraordinary experience" (1). Williams returns to a diagnostic framework: disease is extraordinary experience that must be comprehended and articulated in order to attain a cure. The *Contact* manifesto underlines the double problem of medicine and poetry: seeing and saying.

Williams further defines his sense of contact in "Sample Critical Statement" (*Contact* 4) with a formulation permeated by biological metaphors: "This achievement of a *locus,* Contact has maintained, is the one thing which will put [the American artist's] work on a comparable basis with the best work created abroad. Before the approach to anything of a serious character there must be this separate implantation of the sperm in each case" (18). Williams insisted that art must come from a precise, local experience in order to achieve universality. He then appeals to a sensibility of disease, paralleling illness and tradition; "Nothing will be forwarded, as it is persistently coughed at us for our children to believe, by a conscious regard for traditions which have arrived at their perfection by force of the stimuli of special circumstance foreign to us, the same which gave them birth and dynamise them to-day" (18). The sense of the local is the sensory. The artist must seek out a local "color or contour" (18), an object to present— shoes beneath the sink, a soda sign, or an old goose. If the local is violated, if something is ripped from contact with the senses, it becomes an inarticulate object. It cannot speak its own truth (through the rhetoric of clarity). For Williams it is like a "severed hand" (19)—an image not only medical but also sightless and unable to touch.

This sense of art is a reenactment of the ongoing medical debate between local practitioners and laboratory or public health physicians. Before scientific medicine isolated specific causal agents (in the late nineteenth century), the "specificity" of disease was conventional medical wisdom. Basically, specificity was "an individualized match between medical therapy and the specific characteristics of a particular patient and of the social and physical environments."[33] That conception of disease and therapy was officially rejected in the twentieth century in favor of laboratory determination, but it remains present in medical discourse. Practicing physicians, particularly in Williams's time, saw much more of their patients than their isolation on a hospital ward or the markings on a chart or lab report. Environmental and social issues might not figure in the official notion of disease as caused by a microbe, but the experience of the physician taught him to take those specifics into account.

In the American Grain, published several years after *Contact,* bemoans the loss of contact. In Williams's view, the pioneers huddled together on the edges of the New World without trying to touch or embody it as knowledge. He compares Catholic missionary methods with Protestant, showing the appeal of Protestantism because of its openness (a Bible translated into the Indian language) but then damning the teachers for not allowing the Indian to touch them. Williams points to this lack as a fundamental problem of America today: "From lack of touch, lack of belief. Steadily the individual loses caste, then the local government loses its authority; the head is more and more removed. Finally the center is reached—totally dehumanized, like a Protestant heaven. Everything is Federalized and all laws become prohibitive in essence" (*IAG* 128). For all its potential ambiguity and difficulty, contact (direct sensory apprehension) is the only thing that can stand up to the dehumanizing, centralizing forces of abstraction. Williams reenacts the Curtius/Vesalius debate, arguing that the only thing that can triumph over hidebound universals is the local.

It is ironic that in medicine new technologies enabled reformers to throw off tradition and advocate contact. Stanley Joel Reiser's analysis of medicine and technology traces this movement: "The practice of dissecting bodies to find physical evidence of disease began to transform some eighteenth-century physicians from word-oriented, theory-bound scholastics to touch-oriented, observation-bound scientists."[34] Nevertheless, as Laënnec's motives for inventing the stethoscope demonstrate, new technologies can also deny close contact. The development of aseptic practices brought with it rubber gloves and sterile gowns. Various equipment (the laryngoscope, Wilhelm Röntgen's X-rays, and today's MRI scanners) allows physicians to see the body more clearly, but often at the cost of no longer being able to touch it or even to speak with the patient. In medicine, technology enabled the rejection of theory but did not necessarily provide contact.

Williams was sympathetic to the machine age. He championed "mechanical" artists (such as Charles Sheeler), reviewed George Antheil's *Ballet mechanique* favorably, and even asserted in his prologue to *The Wedge* that a poem was a machine made of words.[35] Still, in the "Jacataqua" chapter of *In the American Grain*, machinery is disparaged according to the principles of contact:

> Deanimated, that's the word; something the sound of "metronome," a mechanical means; Yankee inventions. Machines were not so much to save time as to save dignity that fears the animate touch. It is miraculous the energy that goes into inventions here. Do you know that it now takes just ten minutes to put a bushel of wheat on the market from planting to selling, whereas it took three hours in our colonial days? That's striking. It must have been a tremendous force that would do that. That force is fear that robs the emotions; a mechanism to increase the gap between touch and thing, *not* to have a contact. (*IAG* 177)

It is fitting here that Williams covertly invokes the third of Pound's principles for imagists: "As regarding rhythm: to compose in the sequence of the musical phrase, not in sequence of a metronome."[36] That rule aligns technology with tradition (strictly regular verse), showing how it denies the local or the improvisational expressed in music and dance. Williams feared a poetry that ignored its own locality and lost itself in abstraction. In a way that parallels much medical history, he sets up against the theoretical his ideal of clarity and, failing that, advocates contact with the particulars of the world. His true poetic object must be free of theoretical or traditional categories and enter the "new world naked" (*I* 95).

CHAPTER 3

A Theater of Proof

Observation and experiment are subject to a very popular myth. The knower is seen as a kind of conqueror, like Julius Caesar winning his battles according to the formula "I came, I saw, I conquered." A person wants to know something, so he makes his observation or experiment and then he knows.

—*Ludwik Fleck*

Culture is the flowering of the effort to select. Selection means rejection, pruning, cleansing; the clear and naked emergence of the Essential.

—*Le Corbusier*

The spectacle is not a collection of images, but a social relation among people, mediated by images.

—*Guy DeBord*

The site for the production of knowledge in modern science contributes to and depends upon an ideology of clarity: the belief that one can see and understand an object unmediated by language or theater. In medicine, knowledge is produced at the patient's bedside, in the laboratory, or in the hospital ward. A physician must learn to read the body, understand its signs, and act on a plausible interpretation of those signs. Consequently, most of medicine's technologies and practices are designed to produce stark, readily recognizable differentials. Steven Shapin, discussing the presentation of objective knowledge in seventeenth-century British science, notes "the simplest knowledge-producing scene one can imagine in an empiricist scheme would not, strictly speaking, be a social scene at all. It would consist of an individual, *perceived as free and competent,* confronting natural reality outside the social system" (emphasis mine).[1] Medical empiricism depends upon the erasure of subjectivity and society. It is a celebration of sight. The empiricist dream fails on three points, however: (1) cognitive cate-

46

gories are socially and linguistically constructed; (2) knowledge must not only be visible but also expressible; and (3) the production of a clinical situation or a laboratory truth is inherently dramatic. This chapter explores primarily the implications of the third point.

Ludwik Fleck notes that "the achievement of vividness in any knowledge [*eines Wissens*] has a special inherent effect. A pictorial quality is introduced by an expert who wants to render an idea intelligible to others. . . . But what was initially a means to an end acquires the significance of a cognitive end."[2] Fleck attacks the old saw "seeing is believing" by exposing the slippage that occurs when simple, sensory cognition becomes the primary mechanism for truth production. Although medical training is tactile, olfactory, aural, and visual, most of its technologies tend toward the visual (textual). Much effort is put into the clear display of easily differentiated signs. In *The Clinical Training of Doctors,* Pinel stresses the importance of the hospital for teaching because it allows "selecting a small number of patients for didactic purposes and grouping them on teaching wards."[3] This educational pattern creates a situation where bodies can be read and differences noted with a minimum of contextual interference. In "How the Poor Die" George Orwell poignantly describes the practice. Unlike the other patients, Orwell was given particular attention by the doctors and students because he was "an exceptionally fine specimen of a bronchial rattle."[4] Consequently, while the patients around him died, he was surrounded by young doctors waiting for their turn at the stethoscope.

After Florence Nightingale's reform movement, most American hospital wards were more open, airy, and well lit. She defined the minimum space for a bed to occupy as eighteen by twelve feet.[5] In teaching hospitals, that space was sufficient for a reasonably large audience of students to witness the spectacle of disease (see figure 2, taken from *The Scope,* Williams's medical school yearbook). In addition, most teaching hospitals were equipped with clinical amphitheaters—places for the displaying of pathology (see figures 3, 4, and 5, also taken from *The Scope*). These sites play an important role in the production of medical truth. Enlightened, scientific medical training conducts its business free of superstition in the open space of a theater of proof.

By the late nineteenth century, a new site of knowledge produc-

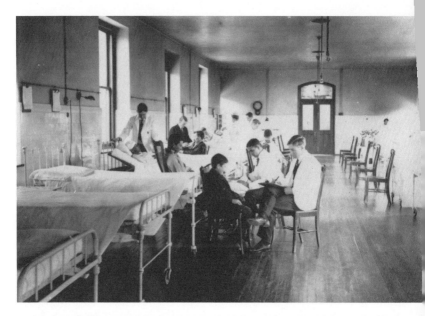

Fig. 2. "Medical Ward Class," *The Scope,* 1906. (Courtesy of The University of Pennsylvania Archives)

Fig. 3. "Old Blockley Clinic," *The Scope,* 1906. (Courtesy of The University of Pennsylvania Archives)

Fig. 4. "The Clinic at Pennsylvania Hospital," *The Scope,* 1906. (Courtesy of The University of Pennsylvania Archives)

Fig. 5. "Lecture Room," *The Scope,* 1906. (Courtesy of The University of Pennsylvania Archives)

tion was added to medical education and practice—the laboratory. William Welch, in his Harvey Lecture on medical education in America (1916), said, "I believe so firmly in the laboratory method in imparting that kind of knowledge which is really vital, a knowledge that gives power."[6] Clearly Welch is referring to the scientific power of medicine to save lives, but the laboratory, like the amphitheater, also has both social and rhetorical power. The laboratory does not represent a radical break from the clinical method. Rather, it extends the ideology of clarity to the cellular level, shrinking the theater of proof's stage to a microscope slide.[7] Few would deny that laboratory medicine involves the control and manipulation of actors in a medium. Experiments and tests are designed so that the knowledge desired becomes visible to the observer. The clinical method echoes that design on a macroscopic level by reading the manifest and latent text of the body. The only difference is that the actors on the stage are not usually manipulated with as much impunity as a microbe. The ideal clinical method is essentially passive: nonaggressive, diagnostic, and on the whole, without much therapeutic value. As Foucault says, "the observing gaze refrains from intervening: it is silent and gestureless. Observation leaves things as they are; there is nothing hidden to it in what is given."[8] On an epistemological level, however, both laboratory medicine and the clinical method are anything but passive. The gaze constitutes and transfixes the object (patient or cell) and creates a dramatic scene of both viewer and viewed. The power to construct, maintain, and propagate those relations depends on the control of both object and viewers and the active suppression of those viewers' awareness of the dramatic mechanism.

According to Shapin, "the physical and the symbolic siting of experimental work was a way of bounding and disciplining the community of practitioners, it was a way of policing experimental discourse, and it was a way of publicly warranting that the knowledge produced in such places was reliable and authentic."[9] Claude Bernard, an early advocate of laboratory medicine, ends his discussion of vivisection with a telling comment: "It is impossible for men, judging facts by such different ideas, ever to agree; and as it is impossible to satisfy everybody, a man of science should attend only to the opinion of men of science who understand him, and should derive rules of conduct only from his own conscience."[10] Shapin (and other historians and sociologists of science)[11] shows that these rules of conduct are not specifically derived from scientists' conscience but are part of the coded behavior of laboratory life. Tellingly, Bernard's appeal to truth as the province of men who understand the particular science runs counter to the empirical ideal of the laboratory as place for the production of free, objective knowledge. Instead, those objects are the product of socially conditioned cognition and are often not reproducible.[12]

In *The Pasteurization of France* Bruno Latour examines the power of Louis Pasteur's laboratory to define objectivity, standards of practice, and mechanisms of measurement. According to Latour, even though Pasteur established clear methods and protocols, he did not achieve universal applicability, but instead succeeded in producing a portable laboratory that he could move onto the farm in order to produce the same results by using the same methods.[13] In other words, Pasteur did not "discover" a cure for various diseases but rather found a way of controlling them through alliances along fragile networks.[14] Pasteur developed his power by staging highly controlled "miracles," such as the prevention of anthrax at Pouilly le Fort: "Having captured the attention of others on the only place where he knew that he was the strongest, Pasteur invented such dramatized experiments that the spectators could see the phenomena he was describing in black and white. Nobody really knew what an epidemic was; to acquire such knowledge required a difficult statistical knowledge and long experience. But the differential death that struck a crowd of chickens in the laboratory was something that could be seen 'as in broad daylight.' "[15]

Pasteur's laboratory makes the invisible visible. He detaches the object from the opacity of its context and displays it as a yes-or-no differential, a process that is the royal road to laboratory truth.[16] Latour notes:

To "force" someone to "share" one's point of view, one must indeed invent a new theater of truth. The clarity of Pasteur's expositions is not what explains his popular success; on the contrary, his movement to recruit the greatest possible number of allies explains the choice of his demonstrations and the *visual* quality of his experiments. "In the last instance," as one used to say, the simplicity of the perceptual judgement on which the setting up of the proof culminated is what made the difference and carried conviction. Pasteur was not stinting in the laboratory and outside in concentrating interest and discussion on a few extremely simple perceptual contrasts: absence/presence; before/after; living/dead; pure/impure.[17]

Pasteur succeeded in producing an ideal theater of proof where truth could be displayed for all who come to see as a clearly manifested differential, and more importantly, the apparatus of presentation was not readily perceivable. Instead, the visitors saw both dead and live sheep in a pen.

It could be argued that for Williams, simple sensory cognition became an end unto itself, and his poetic practice was the recording of minute differentials. But that statement misses the full impact the theater of proof has on his work and on readers' response to it. Williams spent a year studying in Leipzig in 1909 and later in Vienna—an experience that found its way into his novel *A Voyage to Pagany.* While on his 1924 tour of Europe, which included his study in Vienna, he kept a journal later published as "Rome."[18] There he interrupts some notes on a medical lecture regarding the progress of disease with a paragraph similar to the argument in *The Embodiment of Knowledge:* "In the middle ages, they revered knowledge, the few who possessed it felt they had a treasure, it radiated through their lives giving clarity—range, a PLEASURE" (24). Williams characteristically relates knowledge to pleasure, but he also aligns it with clarity. His comment takes on increased significance given its context in the lecture notes. Williams's studies in Vienna (as described in *A Voyage to Pagany*) were in classical clinics. He attended the teachers on their rounds, observing closely the various cases, striving to understand the symptoms of disease and to see illness clearly.

In *A Voyage to Pagany* Dev Evans (Williams's alter ego) encounters the American members of his profession: "But which among them is intent to be clear, to straighten out the muddles of misapprehension which enfold them, to have it straight, clean; to know, to have a light cast over the whole? What is American medicine? A hodge-podge of procedure, kindly enough but no head nor tail to it, no wish to seek clarity in that mass" (*VTP* 148). Ironically, European medicine is praised for the very thing for which Williams would often damn Europe: "At once Dev began to get that sense of beauty in arrangement, that fervor which the continental scientific method, built upon their aristocratic thought, had engendered" (*VTP* 152). The novel expresses the rapture Evans (and, one must assume, Williams) feels in the presence of clearly articulated medicine. He spends his time worshiping in the theater of proof:

> There was no feeling but the presence of the truth. It hurt an American. Old, deformed, or young and unfortunate, they came there and were stripped to be inspected. The gross nose of Cyrano, the girl with the warty face, the peasant with deep ringworm of his beard. One especially Evans was fascinated to see—a girl, barely fifteen—with the pock. Poor child, she was brought in cowering, the tears streaming down her face from anguish and shame, her body marked all over with recent syphilis. Kern patted her, but there she stood and was turned and inspected—studied while she cried and bit her lips. It seemed pitiless, but there it was. She was taken out to be cured.
>
> Tongues were projected, men were turned upside down, women were exposed in minutest detail to the last recess, eyes, nose, mouth, fingers, toes; ulcerated, blistered and stained. Pocked and eaten, swollen and bleeding—nothing remained that was not seen, described and—a clarity put upon it. (*VTP* 155)

The activity of the theater of proof is brutal. It can "hurt an American," but in order to gain knowledge, one must look, and what one sees is not confused by inadequate representation: it is simply there. The knowledge produced by objective display is true because no discourse is more *dans le vrai* than that which appears to be unmediated by language—that which appears not to be discourse at all.

This careful staging of truth depends on a materialist epistemology—a belief in the possibility of clear vision and a virtually transparent language. Discussing clinical medicine, Foucault comments: "Over all these endeavors on the part of clinical thought to define its methods and scientific norms hovers the great myth of a pure Gaze that would be pure Language: a speaking eye."[19] The mechanisms of a theater of proof suppress the opacity of language and hold out the possibility that articulation can be transparent. Similarly, inscription devices are developed in the laboratory that enable the organism under study to write for itself—writing that is supposedly not open to interpretation but instead is pure clarity. Williams's own version of this is the human body, which ideally is opened to the gaze and remains legible. In a review of *The Human Body* he writes, "Dr. Logan Clendening has written a book for us about the human body that is lucid, engaging and full of valuable information. It seems really the body itself speaking, a very old, very certain, distinctly Rabelaisian and absolutely unflustered body, looking out through two eyes, a quick brain back of them, at some of the shows of the world" (*I* 359). He describes a dual movement. The body is displayed in such a way that it reveals its own truth, but at the same time, it watches the "shows of the world." While under surveillance, Williams's body keeps observers arrested by its own gaze. For Williams, this was not just a medical but also a poetic ideal. Discussing the source of poetry, he claims, "it is the deeper, not 'lower' (in the usually silly sense) portions of the personality speaking, the middle brain, the nerves, the glands, the very muscles and bones of the body itself speaking" (*Int* 98). Williams's sense of poetry is at times clearly aligned with the empiricist dream of a transparent language that merely assists in bringing forth the truth, a truth that is not so much told as it is presented, either by Foucault's speaking eye or Williams's speaking body.

Foucault goes on to say that "clinical experience represents a moment of balance between speech and spectacle. A precarious balance, for it rests on a formidable postulate: that all that is *visible* is *expressible,* and that it is *wholly visible* because it is *wholly expressible.*"[20] With his usual magisterial style, Foucault exposes the poverty of empiricism. Not only is truth reduced to that which can be seen, seemingly unmediated or manipulated by theater, but it is also restricted to that which can be articulated. Unwilling to adopt a simplistic empiricism, Williams on numerous occasions adds imagination to the mix: "In the composition, the artist does exactly what every eye must do with life, fix the particular with the universality of his own personality—Taught by the largeness of his imagination to feel every form which he sees moving within himself, he must prove the truth of this by expression" (*I* 105). The presence of the author's personality or imagination guarantees that the observation is no mere recording of incidental detail. Instead, it is a truth produced through the alchemy of the mind, but Williams acknowledges in his final phrase the importance and difficulty of articulation.[21]

Williams was clearly aware of this problem of language. As a physician, he could misread a legible body (as is documented in "Jean Beicke"), and much of his poetry takes language as its subject (particularly *Paterson,* book 1). But to focus simply on problems of articulation is to ignore the "rhetorical" power of

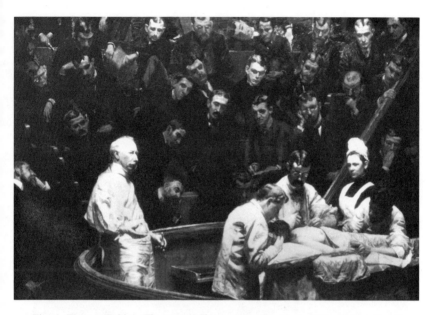

Fig. 6. Thomas Eakins, *The Agnew Clinic,* 1889. (Courtesy of The University of Pennsylvania Art Collection, Philadelphia, Pennsylvania)

space and mechanisms of presentation. Every day when Williams entered the Medical Laboratories Building at the University of Pennsylvania Medical School, he would pass Thomas Eakins's painting of Dr. Hayes Agnew's surgical clinic (figure 6). That painting and its more famous predecessor, *The Gross Clinic* (figure 7), are the topographical embodiments of the theater of proof. Both depict a physician, his assistants, and a patient occupying center stage in a surgical amphitheater crowded with observers eager to see both the techniques of surgery and the truth of disease. Eakins himself was well trained in anatomy and, in 1876, became chief preparator/demonstrator for the surgeon W. W. Keen, who lectured at the Pennsylvania Academy of Fine Arts.[22] Consequently, he understood methods for staging empirical presentations. He was familiar with the architecture of the clinic, the disposition of instruments and assistants, problems of lighting, and the importance of clearly focused observation by all participants in the drama.

The paintings themselves diffuse this focus a bit, since the viewers look at both the patient and the represented doctor. This shift-

Fig. 7. Thomas Eakins, *The Gross Clinic,* 1875. (Courtesy of Jefferson Medical College of Thomas Jefferson University, Philadelphia, Pennsylvania)

ing out from the medical to the artistic scene closely parallels the experience of reading Williams's work. There readers see and hear the doctor/narrator seeing and hearing the objects of his world and, consequently, focus alternately between the perceiver and the perceived. Similarly, Eakins's paintings tend to include the viewer in the amphitheater as part of the audience, yet at the same time, distance him or her from the scene by the sheer violence of the objective presentation (another phenomenon familiar to readers of Williams).

The Gross Clinic focuses on the operation, a presentation of disease. The only part of the patient visible is his thigh, from which a piece of dead bone (the result of osteomyelitis) is being excised. Indeed, there is no way to tell from evidence internal to the painting that the patient is male. Eakins uses a dark palette, so the observers in the gallery are barely visible (an effect furthered by the painting's age and some early neglect). The painting depicts surgical practice's dependance on natural lighting through sky-lights, which is directed onto the stage of the theater and accounts in part for the intensity of the light on Gross's brow and the pa-tient's thigh. Medical knowledge in this scene is produced by the gradual, minute unveiling of the body to reveal the object of dis-ease (here a piece of bone and some granulations). In the audi-ence, all efforts are bent toward seeing that object and conse-quently understanding its truth.

The Agnew Clinic depicts a similar architectural setting and focus. In contrast to the earlier painting, Eakins's palette is paler and the light more diffuse, in keeping with advances in surgical technologies by 1889 to include artificial lighting.[23] By this time, aseptic practices had become accepted; consequently, the team wears white scrubs, but they do not yet wear masks or gloves. In a position similar to that of Dr. Gross, Agnew has paused from his work, but he does not avert his gaze. All figures watch a woman undergoing thoracic surgery, but unlike *The Gross Clinic,* the viewer's focus is not on the incision; rather Eakins seems more concerned with detailing the technical scene of the operating the-ater.[24] The observers are more visible and the physical disposition of the amphitheater is clearly represented. The stage is bounded by a wooden barrier, which focuses the viewer not only on the operation but also on the mechanism of presentation. The observ-ers are separated from the scene of disease, witnessing it at a safer distance than in *The Gross Clinic* (modern amphitheaters place the audience much higher and usually behind glass walls). The viewer is also placed at a greater distance from both the incision and the scene. This effect is furthered by the position of the painting in the Medical Laboratories Building. Hung above the landing of the large staircase, the painting can be viewed comfortably only from a balcony overlooking it. Consequently, the viewer's position is as if he or she were on the upper tiers of the operating theater.

These differences enable a glimpse into the workings of the theater of proof. *The Gross Clinic* embodies its ideal form because the viewer's eye is drawn irresistibly to the point of incision and to Gross's head and hand. The surgeon's scalpels and assistant's probes are adjunct to and participating in the unveiling of what seems a virtually unmediated form. All else is lost in shadow and must be sought out by the viewer anxious to look away from the violence of the scene. *The Agnew Clinic*'s lighting and disposition soften the viewer's clarity of focus. The eye is again drawn to the supervising physician and to the patient, but the exact nature of the operation remains concealed. This allows the viewer to look about at the details of the immediate scene of medical knowledge and reveals the apparatus of objectivity. The bounded space of Agnew's operating area serves two functions. Unlike *The Gross Clinic*, where the instruments are sprawled out on a table in the foreground and the doctors seem to be wearing street clothes, the figures within the middle circle are sanitary (more or less) and the instruments are in a closed case. In addition, the architecture constructs a hierarchy of vision. The doctor and his assistants are closer to the truth than those in the gallery. Although positioned at the edge of the circle's boundary, Agnew has a clear line of vision at the incision and all the participants remain under the watchful eye of the nurse who, unlike the female figure in *The Gross Clinic*, does not avert her gaze, but instead seems to provide a control and authority lacked by the other figures present.[25]

The viewer, being placed on the other side of the amphitheater, is not privileged with clear vision, but neither are some of the observers in the theater, who must crane their necks to see. *The Agnew Clinic* dramatizes how objective presentations are, in a sense, made less clear by the very methods necessary for the presentation—the physical scene, the positioning of participants, and an ideology that focuses on the single unveiled detail that should, in some way, explain numerous diverse phenomena. Steven Shapin and Simon Schaffer explore this problem as it was encounter by Robert Boyle and his followers when they attempted laboratory proofs for the Royal Society. By requiring one to be a member or an invited guest to attend a presentation by the Royal Society, they were guaranteed an educated audience who already knew how to see and consequently recognize objective proof when they saw it. This requirement points out the paradox of the theater of proof. Ideally, it is supposed to show and, by showing, produce knowledge, but in order for the object to be seen, the members of the audience must already know what to look for. In other words, they must already have seen the object they are supposed to be discovering. To echo Latour, the objects are called upon to settle the controversy only *after* the controversy has been settled. From this perspective, the representation of the scene of knowledge (textually or pictorially) is an enactment (and displacement) of an original demonstration, which is always a displacement of prior repetitions. As if to underline the importance of a well-trained audience, in both the *Gross* and *Agnew Clinics* Eakins peopled his galleries with portraits of famous medical men in Philadelphia and included self-portraits.

The harsh realism of *The Gross Clinic* denied it prominent display in the art galleries of the Philadelphia Centennial exhibition. Instead it was hung in the "U.S Army Post Hospital" among the medical exhibits. *The Agnew Clinic,* while not as harsh, has nearly always found its home in a medical setting rather than public display. That circumstance calls attention to another facet of the theater of proof: to constitute someone or something as an object—to subject it to the gaze of a presenter and an audience—carries with it an element of brutality. As Williams said of the Vienna clinics, presentation "hurt an American" (*VTP* 155). Discussing *The Gross Clinic,* Michael Fried notes that the woman with averted eyes "leads me to imagine that the definitive realist painting would be one that the viewer literally could not bear to look at: as if at its most extreme, or at this extreme, the enterprise of realism required an effacing of seeing in the act of looking."[26] The scene depicted in *The Gross Clinic* would make most viewers a trifle squeamish, but Fried's point extends beyond the particulars of an operation to the actions of the theater of proof in general. The constitution of the scene of objectivity is, in itself, violent.

A brief look at the work of a painter who does not usually represent the human form, Charles Sheeler (Williams's good friend and fellow American artist), helps explain this phenomenon.[27] After his early abstractions of Pennsylvania barns, Sheeler turned to photography, working for a time commercially taking pictures of, among other things, New York skyscrapers, Henry Ford's River Rouge automobile plant, and various types of machinery. In discussing photography as an appropriation of images, Susan Sontag claims that "there is an aggression implicit in every use of the camera."[28] Her idea can be expanded to all uses of objectivity or objectification in a realistic mode. Eakins's own photographs, particularly his Marey wheel photos of nude men moving, are more than simple studies. They reveal what is normally beyond vision by arresting motion and dissecting it almost to the point of fetish. In a cold and disturbing way, they violate the sanctity of the human body. Eakins's clinic paintings depict scenes of human drama and violence while Sheeler paints "landscapes" of machinery virtually devoid of human forms, but both rely on a realist tradition (albeit from different centuries) that objectifies its subjects, rendering them starkly and, on the whole, without sentiment.

That tradition is also evident in the work of other photographers. For example, Karen Lucic notes that Paul Strand "focuses solely on the machine itself, but instead of placing it in an empty field, he shows a fragmentary, close-up view of its parts. [He] emphasize[s] the machines' formal properties above all else, accentuating their assertive geometries, sleek surfaces, and linear clarity."[29] Although she does not emphasize the idea, Lucic's phrase "assertive geometries" is important because it carries with it a sense of the violence one senses while looking at Strand's and Sheeler's machine pictures. Throughout *On Photography* Sontag argues that photography is primarily surreal. One must add that its surreal quality is not an articulation of a dream state; rather, it is the result of a violence done to time, space, and the viewer's sense of continuity.[30]

This effect is evident in Sheeler's late-1930s *Rolling Power* (figure 8) and *Suspended Power.* Both paintings, reproduced in *Fortune* magazine, were criticized in *Parnassus* for their too literal representation and the fact that they "fail to capture the nature of power . . . the soul of the machine."[31] Actually, they represent all too well the nature of power—the power of objectification when it suppresses the mechanism of presentation. They show few brush strokes and little human intervention. Even though *Suspended Power* depicts human forms, they seem ineffective and curiously unrelated to the subject of the painting. These paintings are the soul of the mechanism of the theater of proof, which constitutes an object, traps it by the gaze, and then suppresses its own artifice. Williams says of Sheeler's work: "The essence lies in the thing, and shapes it, variously, but the sensual particularization is the proof, the connection which proves that the senses see a reality. . . . In the particularization the artist gains his authority" (*RI* 144). This, in a sense, summarizes the dynamic of the theater of proof. It is a way of bounding and disciplining both its objects and its observers. It submits both the viewed and the viewer to the mastery of the artist, who constructs the scene but at the same time evades the absolute control of the object or the audience.

In *The Birth of the Clinic* Foucault argues that "the descriptive act is, by right, a 'seizure of being' *(une prise d'etre)*, and, inversely, being does not appear in symptomatic and therefore essential manifestations without offering itself to the mastery of a language that is the very speech of things."[32] This notion of seizure can be extended beyond Foucault's linguistic formulation to include the construction of a site where an object reveals its density to a community of observers. The theater of proof, where all may come to observe the truth, subjects its objects to manipulation and control and polices its observers by training them to see, while at the same time, through sheer suppression of context, it thrusts the object upon them in all its overwhelming materiality. As in Eakins's clinics, the viewer of Sheeler's works is both fascinated by their content and repelled by the starkness of presentation. Realism is a violence we do to objects and, at the same time, a violence we do to ourselves.

Williams's 1938 "Between Walls" is characteristic of his style and exemplifies both the problems and power of the theater of proof:

"Between Walls"
the back wings
of the

                    hospital where
                    nothing

                    will grow lie
                    cinders

                    in which shine
                    the broken

                    pieces of a green
                    bottle
                         (*CPI* 453)

The poem bounds its space carefully. The title and the first three
lines enclose the field of possibility and focus the reader on increasingly specific details. Williams moves from the general "noth-

Fig. 8. Charles Sheeler, *Rolling Power*, 1939. Oil on canvas, 15 x 30 in. (38.1 x 72.6 cm.). (Courtesy of Smith College Museum of Art, Northampton, Massachusetts. Purchased, Drayton Hillyer Fund, 1940.)

ing / will grow" to the generic "cinders" to the specific pieces of a single bottle highlighted by the sun. Just as in *The Gross Clinic* (and to a lesser extent *The Agnew Clinic*), the space is immediately circumscribed, and within that space the reader's focus is directed toward a single, specific detail, but at the same time, as in the theater of proof, the bottle is insistently there—somehow prior to the poem. The hospital setting provides a pathological overlay to the poem (much the same as the opening lines of "Spring and All") and creates a tension between life and death. In this yard, "nothing / will grow" except the green bottle, which, while not animate, provides a flicker of life.[33]

Williams details a scene and presents an object whose truth lies in its material presence. Yet the impact of this seemingly direct description moves beyond simple observation. "Between Walls" is a scene of violence. The cinders have been shoveled from a furnace into this yard, disfiguring the landscape, and the bottle has been tossed carelessly among them.[34] These agents, along with the walls of the hospital, actively police the area from encroachment. Weeds or flowers will not grow; humans will avoid the area. What could be, in a simplistic sense, an urban pastoral produced by a passive gaze, is shown as a violent no-man's-land—a scene, like Sheeler's industrial landscapes, depopulated and forbidding.

But to stop here is to ignore the mechanism of the theater of proof. Because the scene is a hospital and the poem is in a book by Williams, the reader has a double focus—not just on the objects presented but also on the presenter. Williams assumes the role of Dr. Agnew or Gross in Eakins's paintings or of Dr. Kern in *A Voyage to Pagany,* presenting to his eager audience the details he is privileged to see (and produce) in his role as stage master. The reader attends to Williams's voice, inflection, and line breaks because they in some way hold the key to the truth of the scene. In "Between Walls" Williams teaches his readers how to see such an object. As he said in *Spring and All,* he was writing "imagination's book," "I myself invite you to read and to see" (*I* 89). He clearly finds beauty in this stark scene, which most would pass unnoticed, and he invites his readers to become an educated audience, to become active participants in the theater of proof, witnessing the objects he produces.

Unlike a supposedly unmediated presentation of objective truth (the actual operating room or scene of urban desolation), "Between Walls" and the rest of Williams's literary production re-presents an already absent scene. Nevertheless, like Eakins's and Sheeler's paintings, part of the power and authority of those representations is derived from a rhetoric of objectivity—an invocation of clarity and simple, accurate presentation. In his essay on Eakins and realism, Fried argues the centrality of writing to Eakins's work. He notes that the artist's father made a living as a writing master, and that from an early point in his career Eakins depicted the written word in his texts. This phenomenon dates back to one of his earliest paintings, *Street Scene in Seville* (1870). Fried goes on to argue writing's more subtle significance in Eakins's work by relating the obvious authority of Dr. Gross's bloody scalpel to a pen dipped in an inkwell. Here is a gesture repeated (though not as dramatically) in *The Agnew Clinic.* Surely the similarity between the positions in which one holds a pen and a scalpel was not lost on Williams. Neither was the importance of reading the body. In other words, William was aware of the relationship between his authority as participant in the medical theater of proof and his authority as writer. Like Dr. Agnew, he could step back from the wound (or the world) and watch, with his pen poised, ready to inscribe his work.

Fried develops his discussion of writing by arguing the psychological importance of Eakins's father on the painter's work. It is important, however, to note that the details of *Street Scene* do not simply call attention to writing. The painting represents graffiti: writing that is violent—a deliberate defacing of public property and often a direct insult to public morality and dignity.[35] Eakins's representation of writing, while not as shocking or violent as the scene depicted in *The Gross Clinic,* calls attention to the potential for writing, as a material form, to participate in as well as represent violence. In Williams's work, writing, in and of itself, carries with it a level of brutality. The look of the words on the page, cut there by the teeth of the typewriter, isolated by quick line breaks, and bounded by blank, white paper, calls attention to the words as objects exhibited in a highly abstract theater of proof while, at the same time, allowing them to assert the power of their own material, objective status—their own "aggressive geometries."

The rhetoric of "Between Walls" works on multiple levels, but they are all related to the dynamic of the theater of proof. His stark, plain presentation of a bounded space exploits a rhetoric of clarity at the same time that it controls and (partially) masters its objects. The simple language appears to solve the problem of articulation of objective data (the poem is not contaminated by ambiguous references such as "so much depends" in "The Red Wheelbarrow"). The careful construction of both the scene and the poem teaches the readers and viewers how to read and see. The cinders and the bottle imply violence, the mastering of the object within the bounds of the hospital walls exemplifies control, and the sharpness with which the words are incised on a stark white ground echo Sheeler's machine landscapes. All of this is related to William Welch's invocation of the laboratory, which produces "knowledge that gives power." The construction of the theater of proof locates truth in the simple presentation of an object, but carries with it a rhetoric every bit as thick, coercive, and value laden as any densely argued scholastic argument. Its power, paradoxically, resides it its ability to make that apparatus disappear, so the truth can appear as if in the broad light of day, glinting off pieces of a broken bottle.

CHAPTER 4

Feminism, Clarity, and Unveiling

This is really not merely a law of physics, but it is the fundamental law of logic. It is the law of cause and effect: "Any effect must have a cause, and without cause there can be no effect." This is axiomatic and is the fundamental conception of all knowledge because all knowledge consists in finding the cause of some effect or the effect of some cause, and therefore must presuppose that every effect has some cause, and inversely.

—Steinmetz

Layer after layer exposed by certainty of touch and unhurried incision so that so much color shall be revealed as is necessary to the picture I learn that we are precisians—

—Marianne Moore

Slowly but surely childbirth is being lifted out of the realm of darkness into the spotlight of new science.

—Good Housekeeping, *1926*

Because his comments are wide-ranging and often contradictory, it is difficult to draw a clear picture of Williams's attitudes toward gender relations. Women play a significant role in most of his texts and are respected, patronized, adored, and degraded. In 1917 he wrote several letters to *The Egoist* praising the early chapters of Dora Marsden's *Lingual Psychology* for equating psychology with philosophy (or subsuming philosophy under the aegis of psychology, which brings it closer to biology) and then developing a feminist philosophic perspective. He chastises Marsden for ignoring the male standpoint, however, positing a gendered psychology: "With this magnificent achievement to her credit . . . Miss Marsden . . . proceeds, strangely enough, to lose sight of the following fact: that based on divergent sexual experiences, psychology, the general term, is capable of two very different interpretations: male psychology and female psychology, its basic subdivisions."[1] This distinction, based on biological difference, highlights Williams's desire to know women while, at the same time, denying him true access to his object of knowledge.

Harriet Weaver Shaw, the editor of *The Egoist,* asked Williams to clarify these concepts, which he attempted in a second letter. He continues to praise Marsden's work on the condition that it be read in light of his own opposition—the male as engendering force and the female as definite point of action:

> I think it is fairly safe to say that male psychology is characterized by an inability to concede reality to fact. This has arisen no doubt from the universal lack of attachment between the male and an objective world—to the earth under his feet—since the male, aside from his extremely simple sex function, is wholly unnecessary to objective life. . . . Female psychology, on the other hand, is characterized by a trend not away from, but toward the earth, toward concreteness, since by her experience the reality of fact is firmly established for her. Her pursuit of the male results not in further chase, at least not in the immediate necessity for further chase, but to definite physical results that connect her indisputably and firmly with the earth at her feet.[2]

As Mike Weaver notes, both Marsden and Williams were influenced by Otto Weininger's *Sex and Character*—Williams particularly by Weininger's division of psychology into male and female halves—but Weininger's "error lay in that he credited man with the ability to clarify details, while allowing woman only the power to receive 'henids,' a term coined to suggest undifferentiated thought and feeling received in inarticulate form. Williams denied this."[3] Williams argues that women, because of biological necessity, are concrete thinkers, while men deal with airy abstractions. His contention raises interesting problems for a male poet concerned with articulating the concrete details of everyday life and a physician whose livelihood depends on his ability to concentrate on the material symptoms crucial for diagnosis, particularly in a pediatric practice, where the patients do not have language and the abstracting qualities it brings.

Gender issues in Williams's work have been discussed by many critics,[4] but it is useful to look at notions of gender as they are constituted by science and medicine, such as the medicalization of the female body, the attitude of "masculine" science toward the material or objective fact, and the patriarchal function of medical authority in gender relations. An important set of concepts and vocabulary has been developed by feminist theorists in a critique of Western science. Sandra Harding defines the radical feminist position, which "holds that the epistemologies, metaphysics, ethics, and politics of the dominant forms of science are androcentric and mutually supportive; that despite the deeply ingrained Western cultural belief in science's intrinsic progressiveness, science today serves primarily regressive social tendencies; and that the social structure of science, many of its applications and technologies, its modes of defining research problems and designing experiments, its ways of constructing and conferring meanings are not only sexist but also racist, classist, and culturally coercive."[5] The feminist critique of science is divergent, wide-ranging, and also tied to other critiques of science and technology (Marxist, Third World, etc.). A significant text in this debate is Evelyn Fox Keller's *Reflections on Gender and Science.*[6] After examining Francis Bacon's sexual metaphors characterizing the relation of the scientist to nature (his famous "we cannot command nature except by obeying her"), she concludes "the aim of science is not to violate but to master nature by following the dictates of the truly natural. That is, it is 'natural' to guide, shape, even hound, conquer and subdue her—only in that way is the true 'nature of things' revealed. . . . Science controls by following the dictates of nature, but these dictates include the requirement, even demand, for domination."[7] A key issue Keller raises is not simply the attitude of control and domination but also the ability to recognize what is natural, or the authority to declare what is natural and consequently, what is deviant (e.g., the medicalization of homosexuality or alcoholism).

Keller goes on to examine the historical development of scientific "objectivity" as a shift from broader, more holistic versions of science (such as alchemy) to a science governed by causality and the specific detail. "Masculine" science, as it has been and still is practiced, is the relentless drive to seek out nature, to penetrate her veils in order to isolate the *single* principle that governs *her* behavior. That attitude has, of course, met with remarkable success, such as the isolation of and eventual treatment for the syphilis spirochete or the modeling of the DNA molecule, but it is not necessarily the only strategy for carrying out scientific research.[8] In a medical setting, "masculine" science's primary tool is the gaze—the penetration by an actor (usually male) of a passive (usually female) figure. Ludmilla Jordanova describes the 1899 Louis Barrias statue "Nature Unveiling Herself before Science" as the embodiment of this metaphor: "The figure of the young woman is covered except for her breasts, and she raises both her hands to the veil on her head in order to remove it."[9] Elaine Showalter rounds out the scene with an imagined complementary statue called "Science Looking at Nature": "a fully clothed man, whose gaze was bold, direct, and keen, the penetrating gaze of intellectual and sexual mastery."[10] "Masculine" science's primary activity is revealing what lurks beneath nature's veils. As Williams's alter ego Dev Evans would say, "to create is to shoot a clarity through the oppressing, obsessing murk of the world" (*VTP* 116).

In his letters to *The Egoist,* Williams's starting point for his concept of male and female psychology is biological difference. Medical science has frequently been called upon to justify gender roles in society. Cabanis, one of the founders of the French clinical movement, offers the following explanation of women's position in French society: "This muscular feebleness inspires in women an instinctive disgust of strenuous exercise; it draws them towards amusements and sedentary occupations. One could add that the separation of their hips makes walking more painful for women. . . . This habitual feeling of weakness inspires less confidence . . . and as a woman finds herself less able to exist on her own, the more she needs to attract the attention of others, to strengthen herself using those around her whom she judges most capable of protecting her."[11] Jordanova discusses this point: "Although the logic of these arguments was the same for men and for women, there was an important asymmetry in their application, since women's occupations were taken to be rooted in and a necessary consequence of their reproductive functions, teleologically understood in terms of roles rather than organs."[12] In the guise of praising women, Williams often constructed roles based on biological functions and continued to echo the argument of the Marsden letters. In "Men . . . Have No Tenderness" (1942), "the male scatters his element recklessly as if there were to be no end to it. Balzac is a case in point. That profusion you do not find in the female but the equal infinity of the single cell. This at her best she harbors, warms and implants that it may proliferate" (432).[13]

In medical science, the feminist critique involves not simply the "scientific" construction of the female (and male) bodies, but also the fundamental premises of modern medical practice. In obstetrics and pediatrics, the mother and her children are the "objects" of medicine—the "victims" of what can (with little counterargument) be called a patriarchal situation—but the epistemology of that practice (unveiling the object with the instruments of the theater of proof) is also gendered.[14] Working through eighteenth- and nineteenth-century medical history, Jordanova concludes: "There are three aspects to the question of veiling/unveiling. First, we can attend to the veil itself, to its qualities, metaphorical associations, its contrasting uses and meanings. Second, we can focus on what it either conceals or reveals—woman/nature/truth—that is, on what lies behind the veil. Third, we are drawn to consider the very act of looking itself, an act that lies at the heart of our epistemology. All three bear on the relationships between science and gender."[15] The act of looking becomes gendered if it is keyed to penetration, control, and authority. It objectifies nature (and women) in both a metaphorical and a material sense, but it must be tied to an epistemology that grants the perceiver authority. "Masculine" science creates the situation where nature, the material world, the woman, or the patient *want* to be looked at, are willing, though with some reticence, to take off their veils. For this, practitioners must be educated, patient, and respected.

Paracelsus (1493–1541) treats this issue:

> Now they say that when I visit a patient I do not know at once what ails him but that I require time in which to learn it. That is true; the fact that they make immediate diagnosis is the fault of their own folly, for the off-hand judgement is wrong from the start and as the days go by they know less and less the longer the time, and so they make themselves out as liars. But I seek day by day to arrive at the truth and the longer the time the more diligently I seek. For uncovering hidden diseases is not like recognizing colors. With colors the observer sees black, green, blue, and so on; but if they had a curtain in front of them he would not know them; to see through a curtain would require spectacles such as never were. What the eyes tell may be diagnosed at once but it is useless to diagnose that which is hidden from sight, treating it as though it were plainly visible.[16]

The object (disease) is not clearly visible but must, through diligence, slowly be unveiled (seduced). As in the theater of proof, simple clear-sightedness is not sufficient to see an object: careful presentation to an educated audience is also crucial.

Specific developments in medical technology contribute to unveiling in a modern practice. Although the speculum was used by the Greeks, it did not come into regular practice until the middle nineteenth century.[17] In the early part of that century, American physicians were trained to perform digital pelvic examinations while the patient remained clothed and standing.[18] But with the development of the stethoscope, ophthalmoscope, and laryngoscope, as well as the adoption of the speculum, physicians opened the body for inspection by the other senses—particularly sight. Stanley Reiser notes:

Before the invention of the ophthalmoscope and laryngoscope, internal disorders in patients were not visible to the eye, unless the body's surface were violated through surgery. Vision now competed with sound as the doctor's main sensory probe of the human interior. Laënnec had listened for disease; Helmholtz and Czermak looked for it. Each could do so without recourse to the patient's appearance or testimony. The ophthalmoscope and laryngoscope, invented to detect gross structural changes in the body, also represented a continuation of the anatomic tradition to which the stethoscope adhered. This sustained the tendency of doctors to regard illness in terms of discrete, picturable lesions, as a disturbance of one part of the body more than of the person himself.[19]

These instruments allowed the doctor to constitute the patient as a veil hiding the truth of the disease and articulate the doctor's role in terms of vision and invasion. They became explorers of previously unknown territories and used tools designed to make public what had once been private.

The veil, its subsequent penetration, and what lurks behind are remarkably powerful metaphors in Williams's writing. He comments on his admittance into the homes of the lower classes: "I wish Arensberg had my opportunity for prying into jaded households where the paintings of Mama's and Papa's flowertime still hang on the walls" (*I* 9). His oft-repeated search for the beautiful thing is tied to this privilege: "I was permitted by my medical badge to follow the poor, defeated body into those gulfs and grottos. And the astonishing thing is that at such times and in such places—foul as they may be with the stinking ischio-rectal abscesses of our comings and goings—just there, the thing, in all its greatest beauty, may for a moment be freed to fly for a moment guiltily about the room" (*A* 288–89). Unlike the rhetoric of the theater of proof where (ideally) the object is freed of all context and allowed to speak its own truth, Williams's presentation of the private in public carries with it a violation. Readers often have the nagging sense that they are seeing and hearing things better left in the confidence of the doctor-patient relationship. In Williams's texts there is a double penetration: the doctor unveils the patient for diagnosis and treatment, and at the same time, the author unveils a private scene to his readers. This process often reveals a good bit about the unveiler, a point demonstrated in *Paterson:*

> Take off your clothes,
>
> (I said)
> Haunted, the quietness of your face
> is a quietness, real
>
> out of no book.
>
> Your clothes (I said) quickly, while
> your beauty is attainable.
>
> Put them on the chair
> (I said. Then in a fury, for which I am
> ashamed)
> You smell as though you need
> a bath. Take off your clothes and purify
> yourself . .
> And let me purify myself
>
> —to look at you,
> to look at you (I said)
>
> (104–5)

Here the woman's clothes, when removed, should make her beauty attainable, but her face, rather than being the essence of her beauty, is part of the veil. The narrator is "haunted" by its quietness. He wants to understand the feminine but is unsure how to proceed. Williams often tried to capture women through his writing, usually with the sense of urgency and frustration expressed in *Paterson* or in the essay "Woman as Operator": "With woman there's something under the surface which we've been blind to, something profound, basic. We need, perhaps more than anything else today, to discover woman; we need badly to discover woman in her intimate (unmasculine) nature—maybe when we do we'll have no more wars, incidentally, but no more wars" (*RI* 182–83). By proceeding from the premises set down in his letters to *The Egoist,* however, he denies the possibility that man can attain this understanding. A woman is a "corridor to a clarity" ("Baroness" 283), but she is not the object revealed.[20]

In the "Beautiful Thing" section, Dr. Paterson turns briefly to the true problem of unveiling as the avenue to truth—"I didn't ask you / to take off your skin." There are always further impediments to the clear apprehension of reality, and in all experiments or encounters, there is a point where further unveiling violates the object or experience to such an extent that it is not longer visible or viable.[21] Nathaniel Hawthorne explores this problem in "The Birthmark"—a classic treatment of "masculine" science—and Williams, sometimes humorously, raises it: "In the moment of admiration, she leaned back her head and he saw up to her left nostril a THING, entangled in hairs. Oh, wipe out the stain. The memory lingers on. A delicate false balance. We see too much" (*I* 281).

As Jordanova notes, science must attend not just to the object being unveiled but also to the qualities of the veil itself, a problem explored in "Metric Figure."

> Veils of clarity
> have succeeded
> veils of color
> that wove
> as the sea
> sliding above
> submerged whiteness.
>
> Veils of clarity
> reveal sand
> glistening—
> falling away
> to and edge—
> sliding
> beneath the advancing ripples.
> (*CPI* 51–52)

Here the poet's gaze eventually sees the sand glistening beneath; nevertheless, his attention is focused on the water itself, which he ironically calls "veils of clarity." The water is the source of obscurity, yet at the same time it provides a lens through which to see the sand and imparts the glisten. The medical gaze is directed toward the specific object—what Giovanni Battista Morgangni called the "seat" of disease—but it must also attend to the veils. As in the section of *Paterson* discussed above, the doctor drives to find the beautiful thing, but can never penetrate to the absolute center. Veils are stripped away to reveal truth, but at the same time they are what enable vision or create beauty. They are, in Williams's ambiguous phrase, "veils of clarity."

Williams frequently discussed his writing in terms of penetration: "Once a man has penetrated the obscure jungle he is likely to come out on the plateau where he has a much broader vision than he ever knew in the past" (*Int* 71). "He may . . . penetrate with tremendous value to society into some avenue long closed or never yet opened" (*Int* 97). In his letters, the sexual nature of the metaphor of penetration and writing is often more explicit, as Paul Mariani's discussion of a letter to John Riordan shows: "As for Riordan, if he was ever going to write anything of moment, he added, then every word would have to go 'into the socket' and squirt 'its juice deep there.' "[22] For Williams, writing is often aligned with masculine sexual power and is surreptitiously reinforced by the "masculine" world of science and technology. This is not a stable attitude in his texts, however. He sometimes adopts a brash, locker-room pose when uttering his most sexist comments ("The Buffalos," and "A Descendent of Kings"), or he expresses castration anxiety (praising Anaïs Nin's work, he says, "Nobody is slashing at my legs under the table, maliciously, as with so many women who imitate men" ["Men . . . Have No Tenderness," 434]). At other times, he (somewhat ironically) celebrates raw power, as in "The Flower":

> She it was put me straight
> about the city when I said, It
>
> makes me ill to see them run up
> a new bridge like that in a few months
>
> and I can't find time even to get
> a book written. They have the power,
>
> that's all, she replied. That's what you all
> want.
>
> (*CPI* 324)

The attitude expressed in the Marsden letters—that men were only useful for hunting and procreation while women were connected to the particulars of life—is difficult to reconcile with his writing poetry. In his medical practice, he did move into terra incognita, act, and then move on; consequently, he exemplified a "male" psychology. But his careful recording of the concrete details of his life and the lives of his patients shows his "female" side. His own apparent lack of ease with this conflict is expressed in "Transitional":

> First he said:
> It is the woman in us
> That makes us write—
> Let us acknowledge it—
> Men would be silent.
> We are not men
> Therefore we can speak
> And be conscious
> (of the two sides)
> Unbent by the sensual
> As befits accuracy.
>
> I then said:
> Dare you make this
> Your propaganda?
>
> And he answered:
> Am I not I—here?
>
> (*CPI* 40)

It is telling that this poem was first published in the *Egoist,* a journal partially funded by Dora Marsden.[23] Frank Lentricchia's discussion of Wallace Stevens can help unpack some of the issues raised in the poem. Discussing the problems faced by American males writing poetry in the modern period, Lentricchia argues, "The issue of Steven's sexual identity as a writer—his effort to phallicize poetic discourse—is not just related to but just *is* the canonical modernist issue of poetic authority: the cultural power—or, increasingly for the poetic modernist—the cultural powerlessness of poetry in a society that masculinized the economic while it feminized the literary."[24] Williams's response to these modern circumstances was his appeal to medicine's cultural authority. If poetry is a feminine discourse, one way to "phallicize" it is to link it to a "masculine" scientific discourse. Like Stevens, Williams was caught up in the need to make a living, and poetry was not useful in a masculine economy. "Transitional" is a tentative manifesto, since he puts the argument in an anonymous speaker's mouth and then questions "his" audacity, but the poem voices the same sentiment Lentricchia discusses. In American culture, poetry was considered a womanish practice.[25]

If you couple this idea with Williams's assertion in the Marsden letters that "female psychology, on the other hand, is characterized by a trend not away from, but toward the earth, toward concreteness," Williams can be seen as wholly endorsing the ideas expressed by the speaker in "Transitional." Nearly all of Williams's work springs from the local, from the concrete, hence (according to his theory) from his "female" side. In "The Founding of Quebec" he describes Champlain: "To me there is a world of pleasure in watching just that Frenchman, just Champlain, like no one else about him, watching, keeping the thing whole within him with a[l]most a woman's tenderness—but such an energy for detail—a love of the exact detail—watching that little boat drawing nearer on that icy bay" (*IAG* 70). The image of Champlain containing within him a woman's tenderness implies pregnancy (the birth of French Canada), but what is more important is Champlain's occupation: "how carefully he has noted every island, every tree almost upon the way and how his imagination has run west and south and north with the stories of the Indians, surmising peoples, mountains, lakes, some day to be discovered, with greatest accuracy" (*IAG* 71). With little alteration, that could be a description of Williams's own poetic output—one of "a woman's tenderness."[26]

Ultimately Williams's attitude toward gender roles is ambiguous. One cannot simply point to the overtly sexist texts ("The Buffalos," "A Descendant of Kings," parts of "The Somnambulists") and label the man a male chauvinist. Like Stevens (as he is presented by Lentricchia), Williams was wrestling with a world that denied masculine legitimacy to what he esteemed, and his reactions varied from the macho to the androgynous. His vision of Daniel Boone is of a man without women: "Possessing a body at once powerful, compact and capable of tremendous activity and resistance when roused, a clear eye and a deadly aim, taciturn in his demeanor, symmetrical and instinctive in understanding, Boone stood for his race, the affirmation of that wild logic, which in times past had mastered another wilderness and now, renascent, would master this, to prove it potent" (*IAG* 137). Williams as a writer must prove the potency of his writing by aligning it with phallic discourse. At the same time he undercuts that discourse and betrays his own sense of the femininity of poetry with absurd macho swagger[27] or ironic self-subversion.

These issues can be better understood through a closer look at the patriarchal authority of the medical profession. Regardless of technological innovations, patient confession remains an integral part of the unveiling of disease. The patient's opening discourse, which is essentially a liberating gesture, "Doc I'm sick," is also extracted by the physician, "Tell me where it hurts." In Williams's writing the confession does not simply stop with the doctor but moves on to the reader, creating a situation some find unsettling.[28] Williams's narrator confesses his own symptoms, feelings, and failings. He offers the story of a patient's confession (makes public a private discourse by stripping away the veil of doctor-patient confidentiality) and at the same time confesses his own lust and desire to transgress.

Foucault discusses confession and the role it plays in defusing potential transgression in the first volume of *The History of Sexuality:*

> The confession became one of the West's most highly valued techniques for producing truth. . . . It plays a part in justice, medicine, education, family relationships, and love relations, in the most ordinary affairs of everyday life, and in the most solemn rites; one confesses one's crimes, one's sins, one's thoughts and desires, one's illnesses and troubles; one goes about telling, with the greatest precision, whatever is most difficult to tell. One confesses in public and in private, to one's parents, one's educators, one's doctor, to those one loves; one admits to oneself, in pleasure and in pain, things it would be impossible to tell to anyone else, the things people write books about. One confesses—or is forced to confess. When it is not spontaneous or dictated by some internal imperative, the confession is wrung from a person by violence or threat; it is driven from its hiding place in the soul, or extracted from the body. . . . Whence a metamorphosis in literature: we have passed from a pleasure to be recounted and heard, centering on the heroic or marvelous narration of "trials" of bravery or sainthood, to a literature ordered according to the infinite task of extracting from the depths of oneself, in between the words, a truth which the very form of the confession holds out like a shim-

mering mirage. . . . it seems to us that truth, lodged in our most secret nature, "demands" only to surface.[29]

The doctor-patient relationship is intimately entwined in the dynamic described here—a dynamic closely related to the epistemology described by feminist critics of science. Both depend on a truth located within the depths of one's self and potentially ascertainable given sufficient ingenuity. This attitude parallels but at times conflicts with a therapeutic notion of conversation—that the act of talking helps cure what will never be uncovered.

In *The Poets of Reality* J. Hillis Miller notes the "strongly" sexual overtones of Williams's writing, but the subject is treated in more detail by Marjorie Perloff in her article "The Man Who Loved Women." She points out the sexual fantasies and power lust Williams presents in the guise of being a kindly doctor. While Perloff's analysis is perceptive, a crucial question that needs further examination is why "critical commentary on these medical fictions has tended to rationalize their sexual component.[30] In other words, why do readers want to defuse what is clearly sexual domination? Part of the answer lies in a general belief in science as disinterested and consequently free of "human" motives, but medicine's patriarchal authority and the literature of "confession" also figure prominently.

"The Use of Force" is a useful text for exploring these issues. Perhaps the most widely read of Williams's prose pieces, the story forces on readers' conflicting social values, which they must defuse in order to "avert its power." The lack of a clearly drawn setting forces the child into the center of the story with the father as adjunct (she sits on his lap) and the mother as shadow. The doctor, who relies on patient confession for diagnosis, is confronted with absence: "I could see that they were all very nervous, eyeing me up and down distrustfully. As often, in such cases, they weren't telling me more than they had to, it was up to me to tell them; that's why they were spending three dollars on me" (*FD* 131). The girl, the only source of the truth, is not talking, but her silence is laden with meaning. The parent's denial of the child's sore throat confirms the possibility of diphtheria:

> As doctors often do I took a trial shot at it as a point of departure. Has she had a sore throat?

> Both parents answered me together, No . . . No, she says her throat don't hurt her. (*FD* 132)

In a sense, the fear and denial provide the doctor with the diagnosis, which now only needs confirmation—the unveiling of the throat—which takes place in a remarkably unpleasant scene where the doctor forces the child's mouth open in a fit of rage.

If this were simply a case of a doctor saving the life of an ignorant, recalcitrant patient with a fear of disease—the somewhat unpleasant but necessary actions of "masculine" science— "The Use of Force" would be a self-congratulatory vignette, but the doctor's confession creates a strange tension. He is faced with wordless opponents; the girl is mute, and the parents cannot even lie well. Trying to convince their daughter to cooperate, they use all the wrong phrases:

> Such a nice man, put in the mother. Look how kind he is to you. Come on, do what he tells you to. He won't hurt you. (*FD* 132)

> You bad girl, said the mother, taking her and shaking her by one arm. Look what you've done. The nice man. (*FD* 133)

Helping take the throat culture, their physical efforts are as half-hearted and useless as are their rhetorical powers, so the narrator provides the dialogue, justifying his actions to himself (and the reader): "The damned little brat must be protected against her own idiocy, one says to one's self at such times. Others must be protected against her. It is a social necessity. And all these things are true. But a blind fury, a feeling of adult shame, bred of a longing for muscular release are the operatives. One goes on to the end" (*FD* 134–35).

The doctor asserts medicine's altruistic (if somewhat patriarchal) motives, but his justification is weakened by his admission of his own "blind fury." As a result, the story is both sexually charged and violent: it is a rape. The girl, though quite young, is like a picture girl with "magnificent blond hair" (*FD* 131). As the battle commences, the doctor's attitude becomes demonic: "I had already fallen in love with the savage brat, the parents were contemptible to me. In the ensuing struggle they grew more and more abject, crushed, exhausted while she surely rose to magnificent heights of insane fury of effort bred of her terror of me" (*FD*

133). Later he says, "I could have torn the child apart in my own fury and enjoyed it. It was a pleasure to attack her. My face was burning with it" (*FD* 134). Here is the point where Perloff's question—why "critical commentary on these medical fictions has tended to rationalize their sexual component"—looms. Why is the doctor not seen as a thoroughly contemptible cad?[31] He lusts after a child, degrades her well-intentioned parents, and enjoys inflicting fear and pain. The argument that it is all for the child's own good rings false in the face of his overwhelming lust. Yet readers are loath to condemn him.

A key to this dilemma is medicine's cultural authority. In a "masculine" (and class-based) medical science, the physician has the undisputed authority to penetrate the veils—something a young, lower-class patient should respect. The girl, raised to mythic heights by the doctor's own savage vision, can be seen by the reader as a spoiled brat who is not only keeping the physician from doing his duty but also angering him beyond reason. She forces him to abandon his hard-won discursive authority and resort to brute force.[32] Yet that only partly defuses the story. Because of the cultural power exerted by the medical profession, the reader can wish to forgive the doctor for his anger, but his lust, with its sexual overtones, is problematic. What to do with a pedophilic pediatrician?[33] Williams's inversion of the confessional scene by addressing the story to his readers provides an answer. The doctor can be not only forgiven but also exalted because he is honest about his emotions. When the narrator confesses, he is placed in a passive position and becomes "feminized," which can be a source of power. In traditional literary circles (poetry as "womanish" practice) and in the gendered psychology Williams articulates in the Marsden letters, those who are sensitive, unlike bluff, aggressive "males," are in special contact with their surroundings and themselves. As Foucault said, "literature [is] ordered according to the infinite task of extracting from the depths of oneself, in between the words, a truth which the very form of the confession holds out like a shimmering mirage." From this perspective "The Use of Force" is the story of a sensitive person who can prod for, and not shrink from, his deepest instincts and display them without fear. None of these tensions are resolved in the story. The doctor's lust is balanced (somewhat) by the authority of medicine and the power of confession. He makes public the veil over the girl's tonsils and his own private desires.

Both are transgressions: the first authorized by a "masculine" epistemology and the second by a "female" psychology.

A related issue raised in a feminist context is Williams's use of this family's story and their language. Not only does the doctor control the data presented, but he is also the surrogate voice for his patients. Rather than engaging in a dialogue and arriving at a mutual understanding within the broader context of the family, their setting, and the circumstances surrounding their daughter's illness, the doctor "steals" their voices, displaces their language, and provides a monological account of the events. He does not deprive the family of language completely, but the discourse of symptoms is the only one allowed significance.[34] This disenfranchisement is furthered when the narrator of a short story provides all of the voices, and to turn the screw one more time, when the author of that story is also a doctor. In the "Use of Force," no one is allowed to speak without radical enframing, and the narrator/ author presumes to speak for everyone.

In "Purloined Letters: William Carlos Williams and 'Cress' " Sandra Gilbert examines Williams's use of Marcia Nardi's letters in *Paterson,* asking "why male writers would choose to 'usurp' or 'appropriate' women's words."[35] Regarding Williams's work, one must also add the words and stories of his lower-class patients. Although she places *appropriate* in quotation marks in this passage, Gilbert goes on to use the term as if its meaning were unproblematic. Williams's attitude toward language (its use and ownership),[36] however, is often at odds with the authority of the medical voice exemplified by "The Use of Force" and the model of language implicit in Gilbert's formulation.

Language passes through groups and acquires meanings that identify and define those groups. In his ground-breaking study of the meaning of the word *syphilis,* Fleck discusses the formation of "thought collectives": "Thoughts pass from one individual to another, each time a little transformed, for each individual can attach to them somewhat different associations. Strictly speaking, the receiver never understands the thought in exactly the way the transmitter intended it to be understood. After a series of such encounters, practically nothing is left of the original content. Whose thought is it that continues to circulate?"[37] Fleck's question raises several problems. The idea of passing an original thought from person to person is an idealism that ignores the ideological nature of the medium. In medicine, ideally there is a specific message passed between doctors. Their training and inscription devices are designed to suppress any noise in the communication channel and produce stark differentials. This absolute clarity could enable ownership—the doctor's diagnosis and the truth of the named disease. At the same time, admittance to that discourse is rigorously controlled, so members readily recognize each other and interlopers are kept at bay. But, as Fleck argues, language is not a transparent medium through which the truth moves. He makes problematic the idealist (or positivist) notion that there is a "true" message that is somehow corrupted when it is passed on.

Gilbert follows the positivist model when she accuses Williams of appropriating a woman's words (as does the above reading of "The Use of Force"). Her critique depends on a sense of language as private property that remains in the control of its originator so that "unauthorized" use is a violation. From a medical discursive standpoint, that model is efficacious. Doctors do determine which words can be used to name which diseases (or even which words will constitute a "disease" as an entity), a point underlined by "The Use of Force." But Williams's use of Marcia Nardi's letters and his lifelong "appropriation" of the language of "Polish mothers" points toward another sense of language, one that sees it as communal property. Williams attacked the academy because it tried to defend the English language from American and immigrant infection. Part of his motive is a sense that language (meaning) exists as it is used in local context and cannot be owned. Its pristine purity cannot be protected behind the battlements of academic buildings. Yes, Williams "appropriated" the words of Marcia Nardi and his "Polish mothers," but that very appropriation questions the security of the concept.

Gilbert's discussion (perhaps unwittingly) shows a fracture in Williams's theory of language and, at the same time, a problem in the feminist critique of science. Without doubt, Williams relied on a notion of language as private property to achieve some of his poetic effects. His transgression of the line between the private and the public is the most obvious example. The act of unveiling the truth by penetrating to the heart of the object (continent, body, atom) depends, however, not only on masculine aggressiveness but also on notions of private ownership. One cannot be violated unless one already possesses, yet Williams's poetic practice undercuts the idea that language (or the body) is private property.

In *Yes, Mrs. Williams* (perhaps the most obvious example of Williams's "appropriation" of another's language), Elena catches him scribbling down something she has just uttered and says "What are you writing there . . . I don't want you to write my biography . . . My life is too mixed up" (26–27). She later tells an obscene story and comments, "Now don't you go put that in your book— or I won't tell you *anything*" (115). Of course, Williams does precisely what she forbids. He follows the "masculine" science or enlightenment model by unveiling the private details (and language) of an object—here, significantly, the object unveiled is his mother.[38] Consequently, Gilbert correctly points to the problem of appropriation in Williams's work. Yet one of the primary attitudes expressed in *Yes, Mrs. Williams* is antihierarchical (a point elaborated with *Paterson* in chapter 8), and embedded in that attitude is the dialectical opposite of appropriation. Hierarchies are founded on ownership, on the right to determine first cause and later use. Williams often subverts the ownership of any discourse by presenting without comment words once used by others, but which now make up the (not *his*) poem. From this perspective, his violation of the private, appropriation of language, and penetration of the veils is not an act of aggression. Rather, it shows Williams's refusal *on a linguistic level* to recognize an epistemology based on public unveiling of a privately owned space.

Without doubt, the drive to unveil supports a powerful rhetoric in twentieth-century discourse. Revealing a truth hidden by obscurity depends on clear vision and formal authority, but it is also a violation. The resonance of many of Williams's texts and the construction of authority in modern medicine depends on idealizing this elusive truth and the sometimes violent strategies needed to attain it. Generally speaking, Williams's drive for clarity and his exposure through literature of both his patients' and his own private lives can be related to this masculine economy. But Williams's work also contains what he called "the disruptive seeds which will destroy the very hosts who have taken them in" (*SE* 193). His rhetoric depends on a masculinist epistemology that violates the private; at the same time, however, his use of language subverts that boundary and makes problematic all notions of appropriation and violation.

CHAPTER 5

Someone to Drive the Car: Technology, Medicine, and Modernism

Your body is a wonderful machine. You own and operate it. You can't buy new lungs and heart when your own are worn out. Let a doctor overhaul you once a year.

—Journal of the Michigan Medical Society

The modern hospital is a triumph of the elimination of the detrimental and the unessential. Because of its absolute fitness to purpose its operation theatre— like the engine room of an ocean liner—is one of the most perfect rooms in the world.

—Le Corbusier (quoting an advertisement)

The bridge tender wore spectacles and used a cane. And the rotary movements of the bridge was a good example of simple machinery. Write, said he to himself taking up the yellow pad from the seat of the car and beginning to scratch with—

—A Novelette

Perhaps the most transforming technological innovation of the modern period was the Ford Model T. Not only did Fordism revolutionize production and management-worker relations on a large scale, but the inexpensive automobile also transformed the landscape, enabling the development of the suburbs, the garden city, the traffic jam, and the automobile accident. Changes in transportation coupled with new communication systems, electric lighting, heavy industry, and new domestic technologies brought on a different relationship between men, women, work, and the environment. That relationship was embodied in the discourse of the era, which constituted particular attributes of machinery as valuable beyond their specific mechanical applications. Words such as *speed, efficiency,* and *cleanliness* were more than simple mechanical description. An efficient engine was a good engine; hence an efficient poem was a good poem.[1] Many critics (in particular Cecelia Tichi and Lisa Steinman) have discussed at length Williams and technology, but it is useful to look briefly at Williams's relationship to technology from a medical perspective. At the same time that electric light (and its accompanying domestic technologies), the automobile, and the telephone were revolutionizing society in general, the medical profession was undergoing a massive technological shift. With the general acceptance of germ theory and the need for aseptic conditions, medical practice changed rapidly. Treatments that had previously taken place in the home were now dependent on specialized and not easily transportable equipment. That dependence was one of the factors involved in the rise of the hospital, which was being transformed from a place where the poor went to die to a haven of cleanliness and up-to-date, efficient health care.[2] *Efficiency, speed,* and *cleanliness—* terms with tremendous rhetorical effect on the popular imagination—also became the watchwords of medical practice. The nursing profession, at least in part from the prompting of Florence Nightingale, became an orderly, efficient mechanism for the care of patients. Hospitals began to advertise, always displaying their operating facilities in a prominent position. The importance of technological cleanliness was also promoted by the ascendancy of the laboratory—the theater of proof, where the truth of disease was produced in all its clarity. And the car and telephone transformed medical practice.[3] It is not surprising that the discourses surrounding these various changes appear in Williams's writing. Not only was he living them, but he was also able to exploit their rhetorical power.

Early in the century, after a fair amount of defensive posturing, state medical journals began to accept advertising.[4] Many automobile companies simply ran their generic ads in the journals, but some wrote special copy for the doctors. An ad for the Emblem motorcycle has all the watchwords of a typical modern advertisement—"convenient," "quickest," "least expensive"—but it also focuses on the doctor's work: "An urgent night or day call, one that demands instant response, can be instantly and conveniently

Doctor's Delight

More of these cars are used by doctors than all other makes of cars in Milwaukee,

THEY SPEAK FOR THEMSELVES.

SIMPLICITY, DURABILITY AND ECONOMY COMBINED.

Price $750
With Top $800

JONAS AUTOMOBILE COMPANY (State Agents)
724-728 NATIONAL AVE., MILWAUKEE, WIS.
Dept. C.   Tel. 245 South.

CADILLAC MODEL K.

Fig. 9. "The Doctor's Delight," *Wisconsin Medical Journal* 5, 1906–7.

made on EMBLEM MOTORCYCLE."[5] Middleby Auto Company (1911) advertises "The Doctor's Ideal Car": "This good looking car is always ready, is strongly constructed, has a simple engine and will enable a doctor to make his rounds quickly and in comfort."[6] And Cadillacs were advertised as a "Doctor's Delight": "Simplicity, Durability, and Economy Combined" (figure 9).[7]

Drug companies used similar rhetorical strategies. Schering and Glatz advertise Medinal as "a soluble, readily absorbed and promptly excreted, practical, efficient and safe." Parke, Davis & Co.'s 1907 Antidiphtheric serum (figure 10) offers "safety—simplicity—convenience!" This ad appeals to the rhetoric of the machine age and combines with it elements of the machine aesthetic. The syringe is "*admirably* simple in construction" (emphasis mine)—high praise for either a syringe or a modernist high rise. It is a commonplace that simplicity in mechanical construction generally enhances reliability and durability, but as this advertise-

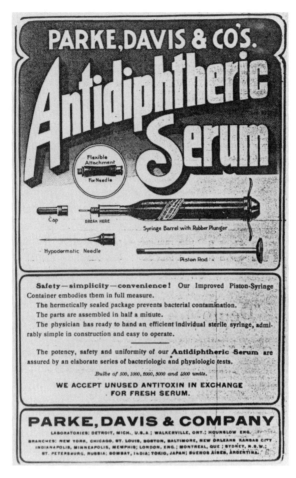

Fig. 10. "Parke, Davis & Co.'s Antidiptheric Serum," *Journal of Nervous and Mental Disease* 34, 1907.

ment shows, simplicity in a modern context carries with it values beyond the merely mechanical. If efficiency is paramount for the new fast-moving physician, Parke, Davis & Co. also makes hypodermic tablets that dissolve in "Five Seconds by the Watch." The modernist doctrine of speed, mobility, clean lines, and clarity most often associated with the Futurists and the Purists or with automobiles and airplanes, was part of the rhetorical strategies directed toward physicians as well. A patient can summon his or her doctor on a telephone, he can arrive quickly by car, and his various medical technologies enable him to act immediately.

Because of his famous definition in the preface to *The Wedge,* "a poem is a small (or large) machine made of words" (*SE* 256), Williams's writing is often compared to machinery;[8] the word *technology* must be used with caution, however. In *Science in Action,* Latour questions the distinction usually drawn between technology and science, arguing that it is merely an explanatory convenience veiling science's dependence on instrumentation.[9] In other words, scientists and their historians wish to see the use of machines as tools to demonstrate already purely formed ideas, not as part of the network of people and apparatuses that is already in place. Latour prefers the word *technoscience* to designate the practices usually designated by the separate terms *technology* and *science,* a useful move because, on an ideological or discursive level, the two practices are closely related if not indistinguishable.

It is also too easy to perceive technology as the physical machine, separate from the forces that produced or use it, or, an even more reductive position, as a force in and of itself. Arnold Pacey avoids these rather naïve senses of the word by making a distinction between "technics" and technology. For Pacey, technics is the purely mechanical part of technology—gears, levers, control systems—while technology includes technics and the social organization of forces that produce and use them.[10] Martin Heidegger takes this point further in his seminal essay "The Question Concerning Technology." He rejects the instrumentalist definition of technology (tools made to perform work toward specific ends) by arguing that instrumentalism depends on ideas of causality without sufficiently examining their foundation. With this argument he rejects the idea of mastery (controlling nature) as the *essence* of technology even though many would characterize that as its guiding *attitude.* Although his difficult argument does not arrive at a final, precise definition of technology, he does claim that "what is decisive in *technē* does not lie at all in making and manipulating nor in the using of means, but rather in the aforementioned revealing. It is as revealing, and not as manufacturing, that *technē* is a bringing-forth."[11] Heidegger rejects simplistic definitions of technology as machinery or as manufacturing and sees its essence as a revealing, a point of some consequence in relation to the feminist critique of science and for a discussion of Williams's machines made of words.

Even though in *The Inverted Bell* Joseph Riddel seems to want to make the case, Williams was not a Heideggerian. Indeed, his sense of technology often tended toward what Pacey called technics or even to technological determinism. [12] And attitudes toward medical technology, while emphasizing unveiling, are usually instrumentalist, etiological, and framed in the discourse of mastery. Still, Williams's writing can be called a technology. He claimed that writers "use words as objects out of which you manufacture a little mechanism you call a poem which has to deliver the goods" (*Int* 69). On the whole, however, his machines do not mass-produce objects, but are instead a revealing, a bringing forth. The essence of Williams's poetry/technology is a "presencing"—a point the following discussion qualifies.

There are two ways of understanding Williams's machines made of words. Either a poem is a *technē,* a revealing-presencing that subsumes Heidegger's fourfold causality, or the language used by the poem is just like mass production: it is made up of interchangeable parts. The point at which these perspectives meet is where a useful discussion of technology and Williams can take place. Williams's work is often like and about machinery (technics), so it resembles instrumentalism: machinery is controlled in order to produce some thing, the poem is controlled by the writer in order to produce something (or *be* some thing). Poetry and technology's essence may be a bringing forth grounded in revealing, but their characteristics are often teleological. This question of control as it relates to revealing-presencing is the question concerning technology that Williams's work forces his readers to address.

His poems often place the narrator inside a car traveling (one must assume) to a house call or the hospital. The opening poem of *Spring and All*—"By the road to the contagious hospital"—is a twofold paradigm of this form in which the narrator catalogs the symptoms of the coming spring as he witnesses them through the window of his car. Thus the automobile (and other transportation and communication technologies) not only lets physicians see things hidden from view but also constructs those objects as symptoms or details by bringing to bear the medical gaze as part of the theater of proof. [13] "Complaint" (1921) is another example:

> They call me and I go.
> It is a frozen road
> past midnight, a dust
> of snow caught
> in the rigid wheeltracks.
>
> (*CPI* 153)

Medicine is the cause of the complaint and the source of the image. Because of his medical practice, Williams must leave his warm bed to tend a woman in labor, but as a result, he is allowed to see the "dust / of snow." The use of the machine (the car) reveals and presences the snow, as does the poem itself. Ironically, his practice and his car place him in a world fit for poetry, but at the same time tear him away. He cannot linger but instead must move on to deliver the child. He has a momentary glimpse—inclusion—but is carried on into the night—exclusion.

The "essence" of the automobile is not, regardless of the claims of the futurists, speed for speed's sake. The instrumentalist view is that the machine is used for specific ends—in this case, to go from point A to point B. Even though transportation technology allows glimpses of worlds unsuspected, it also is firmly focused on its point of penetration—it asserts its own ends. So in Williams's texts, a primary effect of transportation and communication technologies is that they provide momentary contact with the world[14] but at the same time force hurried consumption and onward movement. Williams's poems, which are also mechanisms, afford the same opportunity. A poem that typifies the inclusion/exclusion paradox (the technology of the glimpse) is "The Young Housewife," which relies on a series of passing images: "the young housewife / moves about in negligee," and "stands / shy, uncorseted, tucking in / stray ends of hair" (*CPI* 57). In the first two stanzas, the poem moves from the woman (mentioned in the first lines) through other men who have contact with her (the husband in the first stanza, the fish and ice men in the second) to the narrator, who remains in his moving car. Medical technology[15] reveals and makes present that "beautiful thing," but the physician remains outside looking in. Like wearing a rubber glove in the examining room, he comes in contact but does not touch. The poem itself recapitulates this movement by taking the reader along for a similar imaginative view of the beautiful thing. At the same time, it offers a glimpse of the narrator's psyche through the troubling comparison of the woman to a leaf, which he then crushes with his car in the final stanza. The technology *in* the poem allows the glimpse but no true contact; the technology *of* the poem does exactly the same thing.

Medicine is, in a sense, a form of voyeurism—a carefully constructed social and technical apparatus that allows a privileged few to see things generally hidden from view and at the same time to constitute them as objects to be seen. This voyeurism is perhaps best understood through the history of medical instruments, which are nearly always machines designed to bring the body under the gaze of the physician. Williams's writing frequently exhibits a delight in medical voyeurism and the privileges it confers: "I was permitted by my medical badge to follow the poor, defeated body into those gulfs and grottos" (*A* 288). And his poems, whether of a medical theme or not, have a decided voyeuristic quality, which calls the reader's attention to the voyeurism of all poetry. The technology of reading isolates the reader from other people as well as from the "people" in and the narrator of the text. The experience of the reader is that of the man circling the block in his car.

In a different but perhaps more direct way, the telephone participates in revealing as excluding. "The Simplicity of Disorder" in *A Novelette* is a classic example of Williams's frenetic writing-on-the-run improvisational style.[16] Its narrative is framed by the influenza epidemic of 1929, and its cue is the ringing of the phone. Because of the epidemic, Williams has little time for poetry, yet he revels in the frenzy. The life-and-death circumstances bring a poignancy to the writing.[17] Medically, he can feel assured by helping many through such a horror, yet at the same time, he sees his own ineffectiveness in the face of disease and medicine's inability to curb the epidemic. The physicians can only wait for warmer weather. This emotional complexity is expressed by the title, "The Simplicity of Disorder," which to the scientific mind should read the simplicity of *order.* The title reflects the form, as Williams's improvisations generally defy ordering except in the most complicated and artificial ways.

The phone rings: "Ring, ring, ring, ring! There's no end to the ringing of the damned" (*I* 275). Patients are dying, hence damned, but they are also intruding "in the warm house" (*I* 276) and are therefore damnable. And the doctor is damned to Sisyphian toil not only because of the epidemic but also because of economic necessity. Williams often asserted that he chose medicine so he would be free to write, free from the need to be a starving poet, yet that freedom cost him, since medicine is both an altruism and a commodity. It is an incredibly time-consuming profession and, in the Great Depression, is his only "bread and butter" (*I* 276). The opening lines are an exercise in slapstick telephone humor: "My child has swallowed a mouse.—Tell him to swallow a cat then. Bam!" (*I* 276). The telephone reconfigures disease because it creates a new means of formulating symptoms and methods of diagnosis. He continues the slapstick complaints about his lack of time: "Try as I will the thing comes only when I have one stocking on, the telephone is ringing, my mind is full of difficulties and you have asked me a question. In a flash it comes and is gone" (*I* 294). The irony here is that the medical practice, which provides him with his "contact," also intrudes on his writing time. That irony is evident in a letter to Marianne Moore: "It would all be possible if anyone had sense enough (*vide* Ezra Pound's *Cantos*) to give me a salary for sitting on my tail and enriching blank paper by careful work. But intestinal toxemia and mastoiditis are more important to a prosperous community than impalpable directions and invisible (but damned important) pitfalls, etc." (*SL* 92). He wants to be free from his medical work, yet his ambivalence shows through his language. For all his exotic background—Catholic, Jewish, Caribbean—he is imbued with an American Protestant sense of work.[18] He justifies writing as "enriching blank paper by careful work"—a comparison that parallels his respect for carefully crafted mechanical work (as in "Fine Work With Pitch and Copper").[19] In these meditations the telephone comes to signify both medical practice and the loss of time—a time-saving device that is anything but. From this perspective, the telephone plays a crucial role in the transformation of both medical and poetic language.

"To Close," a late "telephone" poem, brings out the inclusion/exclusion paradox from a different perspective.

Will you please rush down and see
ma baby. You know, the one I talked
to you about last night

What was that?

> Is this the baby specialist?
>
> Yes, but perhaps you mean my son,
> can't you wait until . ?
>
> I, I, I don't think it's brEAthin'
> (*CP2* 232)

The poem has all the immediacy of his earlier "doctoring" texts as well as his delight in the language and accents of his patients, but here, rather than dashing off with his well-stocked medical bag in his Ford flivver, Doc Williams hesitates, knowing he has been mistaken for his son William Eric, who at this point has more or less taken over the practice. This simple poem marks a transfer of power from father to son and carries with it a negation of medical authority. A deeper pathos is the difficulty Williams must have had giving up his hard-won local authority. The telephone and his medical practice have once again given contact, only to deny it.

In "Yours, O Youth," published in *Contact* 3 (1921), Williams accounts for America's success in technological terms: "It has been by paying naked attention first to the thing itself that American plumbing, American shoes, American bridges, indexing systems, locomotives, printing presses, city buildings, farm implements and a thousand other things have become notable in the world" (*SE* 35). In a sense his 1923 *Great American Novel* is a response to that point. It is a text that typifies his writing as and about technology. Although Joe Riddel dismisses it as a "multifaceted joke,"[20] and Vivienne Koch laments its title, careful reading shows *The Great American Novel* as an important discussion of technology and writing.

Nearly all major modern inventions make an appearance: telephones, electric lights, trains, automobiles, dynamos, the quick lunch, and businessmen's time management. He even claims the "heroine is a little Ford car—she was very passionate—a hot little baby" (*IWWP* 39).[21] Consequently, much of the text comments on mass production—the importance of speed, efficiency, and the reduction of waste. But it also applies those standards to words and sentences, inviting the comparison early on: "Words take up the smell of the car. Petrol" (*I* 159). Even his dynamos "make a word. Listen! UMMMMMMMMMMMM" (*I* 162). The novel both discusses and exemplifies standardized manufacture. It is made up of standard parts—bits of stories, conversations, advertisements, business letters, and so forth (interchangeable language)—and it always calls attention to the language it uses.[22] Yet *The Great American Novel* exemplifies Williams's ambivalence regarding modern technology.

Ideally, a machine is designed for maximum efficiency, and only after that point is reached is its manufacture and maintenance standardized. The interchangeable parts fit an already clearly designed apparatus. Claude Lévi-Strauss's distinction between the engineer who designs the ideal machine and the *bricoleur* who cobbles together a machine out of odds and ends reveals the technology of *The Great American Novel* as *bricolage*.[23] Williams's machine made of words is inefficiently designed. It bumps, shakes, grinds, screeches, and halts.[24] This is not to say that it does not produce, but that there is waste. Its lines are not clean or streamlined, making problematic any assertions that Williams wholeheartedly embraced a machine aesthetic.

The Great American Novel also calls into question the role of the human in the operation of this machine. Machine analogies in medicine often reduce the patient to a symptom or a list of parts.[25] Interrupting a description of a Mack truck, "the great and powerful mechanism," Williams mentions "the Polish woman in the clinic, yellow hair slicked back. Neck, arms, breast, waist, hips, etc," (*I* 171). What could have been a paean to her beauty in the tradition of the Song of Songs becomes a list of her parts. She is, like Heidegger's "standing reserve," reduced to a resource that can be exploited by the mega-machine—here the technology of the modern health industry. As Foucault has taught us (in *Discipline and Punish*), viewing people as cogs in a machine does not simply involve the Taylorization of workers. It also means the cooptation of abstractions such as truth and justice to a machine-efficiency coefficient. To produce and consume streamlined cars, you need a docile work force and modern bookkeeping as well as supportive legal systems (what Latour calls heterogenous networks). As Williams would lament, "Card-index minds, the judges have. Socialism, immorality and lunacy are about synonyms to the judge. Property is sacred and human liberty is bitter, bitter, bitter to their tongues" (*I* 199).

The Great American Novel is cobbled together from cast-off parts designed for other purposes; in a sense, no one is in full control. The engineer/author is revealed as an idealism. Williams emphasizes that point by refusing to develop any main characters and subverting any traditional or coherent narrative voice. From this perspective, *The Great American Novel* is a remarkably realistic text. The America it is to embody is *bricolage,* which is the heart of Williams's attitude toward technology. He denies the overarching view of technological utopians or social engineers and celebrates local precision: "But with great dexterity he threw out the clutch with a slight pressure of his left foot, just as the fore end of the car was about to career against a mass of old window screens at the garage end. Then pressing with his right foot and grasping the handbrake he brought the machine to a halt—just in time" (*I* 169).

Among the technologies described in *The Great American Novel* are subways, the quick lunch, and the production of neurasthenia[26] (what George Beard labeled "American Nervousness")—all part of a vaster *bricolage* called the city. Williams is, of course, a poet of the city, but his is rarely made up of gleaming skyscrapers. More often it is muddy back alleys and filthy tenement houses. His at times ambivalent celebration of those alleyways places him in a peculiar relation to the modern urban engineers who saw houses as machines for living and extended that model to city design.[27] Ralph Steiner and Willard Van Dyke's documentary *The City* is a useful point of comparison. Through commentary written by Lewis Mumford (whose work Williams knew), *The City* depicts a threefold urban movement from a nineteenth-century pastoral ideal represented by small-town meeting halls, water mills, wagons, and blacksmiths to contemporary smoke-clogged, rat-infested cities and then looks to the future, to new industrial cities to be built by architects and social planners with vision.[28] This utopia is decidedly technological[29] and draws its rhetorical force from machine metaphors: "Order must come . . . [from] all we know about machines."

There is some irony in Mumford's commentary when set up against a sense of Williams as celebrant of the machine aesthetic. For Mumford (and for Williams at times), modern American cities are vile, smoke-choked traffic jams that reduce their inhabitants to unthinking clods (or "standing reserve").[30] Williams repeats Mumford's descriptions, shows virtually the same scenes, but usually without overt moralizing or utopic yearning (though he does at times desire a purifying apocalypse, a point discussed in chapter 7). Williams's work celebrates precisely the details that Mumford, Steiner, and Van Dyke condemn. "The Great Figure," one of his most famous poems, depicts nearly the same situation as the ambulance scene in *The City,* but Williams glories in the sense of speed, chaos, and wonder, while for Mumford, Steiner, and Van Dyke it is the tragedy of a poorly designed urban setting.

The form of *The City* reflects in part both *The Great American Novel* and *Paterson.* Although there is a clear narrative thread and often heavy-handed symbolism (e.g., the village blacksmith in the opening scene), the film uses quick cuts and advertising and business language, and it relies on the lingering image produced by its frantic pace (particularly in the dystopic section). The cumulative effect, however, is not "the anarchy of poverty" that delights Williams ("The Poor," *CP1* 452). *The City* shows "Chimneys, roofs, fences of / wood and metal" (*CP1* 453), but not as a delight to the observer, nor as a matter of pride for the occupant. Instead the camera seeks out desolation. In a sense, the difference is an effect of different technics and technologies. Williams enters the neighborhoods of the poor through medical technology—his role as a physician come to cure—unlike Steiner and Van Dyke, who come with a camera to document. They are careful to exploit the starkness of black-and-white camera work. Many scenes are barely perceptible through clouds of black smoke and white steam, while the utopic sections are literally drenched in sunlight.

The City offers solutions—alternatives to "the anarchy of poverty"—through machine technology: well-planned communities where both machines and people have their place. Steiner and Van Dyke's technological utopia is a blend of the pastoral ideal, clean-lined kitchens and laundries, well-designed transportation patterns, and carefully isolated but readily accessible industry. It is a vision of an engineered society where people will retrieve a lost humanity while still progressing. From another perspective, however, those people could be viewed as the standing reserve of any technological system. People, houses, and towns become interchangeable parts of standardized production. As Mumford claims, "We can reproduce the pattern and better it a thousand times." Williams's answer to this version of machine utopia is localism. He delights in the working of a small mechanism—bridge gears, automobile levers—but pulls back from an inclusive view of society as a machine. If society is a machine, then for Williams it is *bricolage* and not Mumford, Steiner, and Van Dyke's (or Le Corbusier's) master machine for living.

The real question being raised by these two versions of technology and society (local or universal) is human freedom. In "The Question Concerning Technology" Heidegger argues for a freedom that is, to a great extent, quite similar to Williams's view: "The freedom of the open consists neither in unfettered arbitrariness nor in the constraint of mere laws. Freedom is that which conceals in a way that opens to light, in whose clearing there shimmers that veil that covers what comes to presence of all truth and lets the veil appear as what veils. Freedom is the realm of the destining that at any given time starts a revealing upon its way."[31] In his own rather complicated way, Heidegger dissolves the subject/object dualism in which most discussions of technology get mired. Freedom is not to be had by mastering the machine (the role of *The City*'s urban engineers) nor by being subjected to it (the role of the inhabitants of the technological utopia). Rather, freedom is to be had in the recognition that, while technology's prime purpose is to unveil, that which it unveils is its own unveiling procedures. The instrument can never penetrate the last veil to discover pure presence. Instead it is that which by removing veils (and consequently producing them at the same time) allows us to produce presence as absence—to be included at the same time we are excluded. There is no object of technology, nor a master guiding it. Rather, there are unveilings and reveilings of absent presences on a local level. As Williams would put it:

> It is only in isolate flecks that
> something
> is given off
>
> No one
> to witness
> and adjust, no one to drive the car
> (*CP1* 219)

CHAPTER 6

An Ideology of Cleanliness

Neatness and finish; the dust out of every corner! You swish from room to room and find all perfect. The house may now be carefully wrapped in brown paper and sent to a publisher. It is a work of art.

—Kora in Hell

But despite all the tours and detours, just as jam always returns to the pantry, you always end up by sliding in a little word which isn't yours and which bothers you by the memory it awakens.

—Kierkegaard

This is not romance, Dev. This is reality, wake up! We are caught. Cannot even we keep one thing clean? What are our lives made up of, tell me: bitterness, disappointment—not with each other, nothing to do with any of us—it is inevitable. But not one thing clean. I hate America simply because it is my own slough—but we have found something clean, one small clean spot. And so it must remain: clean, a place to rest our heads on.

—A Voyage to Pagany

Williams often expressed the need for "clean words," which is an idea related to clinical medicine's speaking objects and the laboratory staging of truth unmediated by language, but it is also connected to another medical trope: sterility. Although cleanliness has long been regarded as important in medicine, it did not become a crucial part of practice until the late nineteenth century. After Louis Pasteur (with help from Lazzaro Spallanzani and others) disproved spontaneous generation, the way was cleared for the modern conception of germ theory and the viable use of antiseptic and aseptic practices. Joseph Lister routinized the use of antiseptics (carbolic acid) in treating wounds and surgery, a method eventually achieving fairly broad application. Based on his success, aseptic methods soon followed. These were characterized by the autoclave, disposable sterile bandages, sterile operating room, operating gowns and masks, and doctors who finally washed their hands. Although his essay was met with derision, Oliver Wendell Holmes, another doctor/poet, was the first American to advocate aseptic methods in obstetrics.

Even before bacteriological procedures became standardized (by Pasteur and Koch) and such germs as *Septicemie puerperale* were isolated in the cadavers of women who had died of childbed fever, nineteenth-century reformers advocated close attention to cleanliness and sanitation, particularly in hospitals, which in America up until the late nineteenth century were notorious for their mortality rates.[1] The most poignant cry was made by Ignaz Semmelweis in *The Etiology, Concept, and Prophylaxis of Childbed Fever* (1860). While working in the Allegemeines Krankenhaus in Vienna, Semmelweis noted that the mortality rates between two virtually identical maternity wards diverged widely, concluding after accumulating massive data that the only difference between the two was that one was attended by clinical students and the other by midwives. The students were exposed to the cadavers in the deadroom, from which they returned without washing their hands. Semmelweis instituted a chlorine handwashing requirement and the mortality rates dropped, but it remained for sophisticated laboratory procedures to be developed before the significance of his discovery was to be understood and accepted.

By the late nineteenth century the hospital was becoming more than a place for the poor to die. It was a technological system for the education of physicians and the production of health in the community. In 1859 Valentine Francis's *Thesis on Hospital Hygiene* advocated brick construction, frequent whitewashing of the plaster ward walls, double windows extending from near the floor to a sixteen-foot ceiling, plenty of air and light, water closets and baths by each ward, and special sewer for the slops "so arranged that it can be ventilated, cleaned and examined at pleasure." The deadhouse in Francis's plan would be isolated in a corner of the grounds where it "should be kept in a state of great cleanliness, whitewashed several times a year, [and] fumigated often."[2] Like Florence Nightingale (whose *Notes on Hospitals* Francis knew of but had not read), Francis advocates cleanliness not because of a sophisticated germ theory based on later bacteriological discoveries, but because of a belief in the therapeutic efficacy of fresh air and a generalized sense of miasmic theory (diseases are carried by "infected air").[3] As a physician, Williams was quite aware of problems of sanitation, particularly in his urban obstetric training. He interned at the Nursery and Childs Hospital near Hell's Kitchen, presiding over the birth (and often death) of numerous infants born to the inner-city poor. His later practice in Rutherford and Paterson brought him into filthy homes (described in many poems and stories) to deliver infants and perform surgery. In "Old Doc Rivers" the doctor/narrator describes an operation for a ruptured appendix on the patient's kitchen table. Undoubtedly, the issue of cleanliness was at the forefront of Williams's professional life, and its appearance in his literary discourse is significant.

The rise of the hospital parallels the medicalization of childbirth—a point where patriarchy and technology combine in new and potent forms.[4] Regardless of many protestations, obstetric technology is, if nothing else, invasive. Anesthesia and obstetrical instruments are the machines that most clearly represent patriarchal power and, to this day, remain the distinguishing feature of medicalized childbirth. Williams studied obstetrics at the University of Pennsylvania Medical School with Barton Cooke Hirst, whose textbook he used. Hirst's paternalism is evident in his language: "This chapter deals with the management of a woman in labor."[5] He nods toward the "naturalness" of the birthing process and the nonessential role played by the physician in normal childbirth: "Some consolation, however, can always be found in the reflection that labor is a natural and comparatively easy process, in the majority of cases; that a physician's duty is mainly one of inaction and noninterference."[6] (One must assume he means that labor is easy for the physician.) But his text and the very notion of obstetrics in a medical setting point toward the use of drugs, anesthesia, and instruments.

That tendency is best demonstrated in Hirst's chapter on obstetric operations, which is copiously illustrated with surgical appliances (he designed or modified many) that aid in the extraction of the fetus by the physician.[7] Of course these illustrations are schematic and are for instructional purposes, but their semiology reinforces the physician's position as the active partner in labor. The woman is often reduced to little more than a distended vulva with stumps for legs (figure II). There is a long tradition in medical illustrations of this foreshortening, typified by William Hunter's

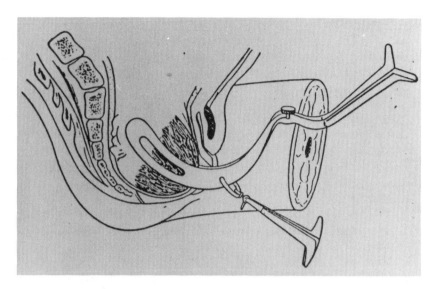

Fig. 11. Barton Cooke Hirst, *A Text-Book of Obstetrics*, 1912, 818.

famous "gravid uterus" series (figure 12), so even though in Hirst the physician is usually only an arm, the hands are strong and are clearly doing the work (figures 13 and 14). Obstetric technology gave physicians an active role in the birthing process, because, as Dr. Walter Channing argued in 1848, the doctor attending a childbirth "must do something. He cannot remain a spectator merely, where there are many witnesses, and where interest in what is going on is too deep to allow of his inaction."[8] Here the apparatus of the theater of proof—a lying-in with witnesses—not only constitutes a specific object of knowledge but also necessitates direct action by the doctor.

The car and the telephone were integral parts of Williams's practice, as were sanitation technologies, but a clear point where sterile machinery makes contact with the very basis of his professional life—the mother and child—remains, on the whole, unexpressed in his literary texts. One exception is the short story "Night in June." Although in many ways typical of the "housecall" text, this story is also a complex meditation on the relationship of technoscience, patriarchy, and childbirth. Barely a paragraph passes that some detail of medicalized childbirth is not mentioned. His failed delivery of the woman's first child involved the forceps. He

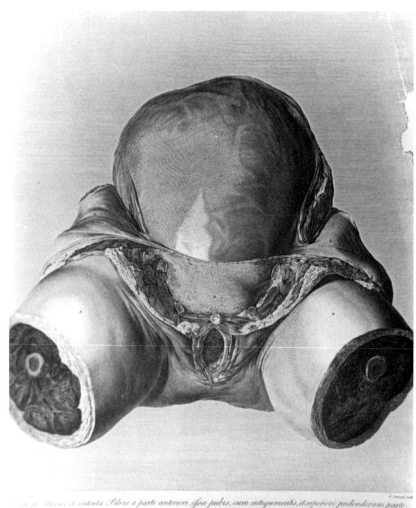

TAB IX. *Uterus et contenta. Pelvis a parte anteriori, ossa pubis, cum integumentis, et superiori pudendorum parte, ... fuerant abscissa, quo cervix uteri, et vesica simul urinaria a protensa in visum incurrerent.*

Fig. 12. William Hunter, *Anatomy of the Human Gravid Uterus,* 1774.

Fig. 13. Barton Cooke Hirst, *A Text-Book of Obstetrics,*
1912, 829.

emphasizes that this visit (her ninth labor) is a home delivery, even
though "one gets not to deliver women at home nowadays. The
hospital is the place for it. The equipment is far better" (*FD* 137).[9]
The narrator is a physician who enjoys the technical aspects of his
job. His medical bag, after three years' neglect (a hospital doctor
has no need of one), still contains the proper material to assist
birth. His description of his syringe resembles the precisionist art
of Williams's friends Charles Demuth and Charles Sheeler: it had
"the manufacturer's name still shiny with black enamel on the
barrel" (*FD* 137).

Yet the narrator is also nostalgic for the days of home birth—for
reproduction under a different mode of production. He delights in

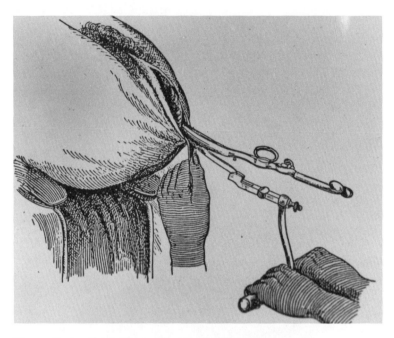

Fig. 14. Barton Cooke Hirst, *A Text-Book of Obstetrics*, 1912, 834.

his patient's "peasant" traits, and the delivery takes on a pastoral quality. With her legs that had "large varicose veins about them like vines," she is "clean as a cow that calves" (*FD* 138, 142). Indeed, the romantic, prehospital setting contributes to the delight most readers experience with the story. It is, in its own strange way, "delicious" (*FD* 140). But the seeming dominance of the pastoral ignores the technoscientific, which, regardless of the nostalgia, triumphs.[10] The passage comparing veins to vines is followed by "everything was clean and in order." The doctor debates with himself about inducing labor with pituitrin: "Science, I dreamed, has crowded the stage more than is necessary. The process of selection will simplify the application. It touches us too crudely now, all newness is over-complex" (*FD* 141). But he gives her larger and larger doses: "But without science, without pituitrin, I'd be here till noon or maybe—what? Some others wouldn't wait so long but rush her now. A carefully guarded shot of pituitrin— ought to save her at least much exhaustion" (*FD* 141). This personal debate is telling since, even though his primary concern is for his patient, he is also worried about using his time efficiently. If, as Tichi argues, efficiency is the watchword of the twentieth century, this physician must also be concerned about wasting his own time. Part of the "deliciousness" of his visit is that he has taken refuge from the life of a hospital practice in this family's home. He is playing hooky.

Nevertheless, the aesthetically regarded syringe does its job, and the story comes down on the side of science and technology, even if the doctor expresses momentary ambivalence: "Oh yes, the drops in the baby's eyes. No need. She's as clean as a beast. How do I know? Medical discipline says every case must have drops in the eyes. No chance of gonorrhoea though here—but—Do it" (*FD* 143). Williams will, at times, subvert the patriarchal power of the physician, but here he follows his mentor, Barton Cooke Hirst, carefully "managing" this female.

Science and technology further the abilities and consequently the authority of the physician over his patients. In no place is that power more conspicuous than in the birthing room, so the building that contains those rooms—the hospital—is the clearest emblem of the new sanitation technologies.[11] The enameled and tiled walls and floors could be cleaned to a sterile brightness and disinfected in ways older structures could not, and the necessary waste disposal equipment, as Francis advocated, was ready to hand. This emphasis on sanitation is illustrated in a 1915 advertisement for the Charlotte Sanitorium's surgical department:

> The table is of the latest model of white enamel frame, with glass and nickel plated steel fixtures. On this the patient can be put in any position at a moment's notice. A large circular glass table is used for the instruments and dressings and can be wheeled to the operator's side where everything is at hand. The glass top stool, medicine and anaesthetic tables are easily placed at any desired point. The floor is tile, the wainscoting of marble with enamel ceiling. The woodwork is in white enamel and everything can be thoroughly cleaned.[12]

The prevalence of porcelain, glass, and nickel plate typifies aseptic technology, but also closely relates to the modernization of the household kitchen and bath. Marcel Duchamp resigned from the committee for the Independents Exhibition (1917) when it refused his pseudonymously submitted "fountain"—a urinal signed "R. Mutt." In *The Blind Man* he noted, "The only works of art America has given are her plumbing and her bridges."[13] Though he meant at least in part to scandalize, Duchamp's claim must be taken with some seriousness. The ideology of cleanliness—its modern form developed by Lister and his colleagues—moved quickly in America from the hospital to the home.

Tichi discusses Williams's shift from romantic maundering to a poetry of the mass-produced image in his 1917 poem "Good Night." The shift is also, in a sense, related to the new sanitation technologies the hospitals were beginning to use at the time.

> In brilliant gas light
> I turn the kitchen spigot
> and watch the water plash
> into the clean white sink.
> On the grooved drain-board
> to one side is
> a glass filled with parsley—
> crisped green.
> Waiting
>
> for the water to freshen—
> I glance at the spotless floor—:
> a pair of rubber sandals
> lie side by side
> under the wall table
> all is in order for the night.
> (*CP1* 85–86)

Cecelia Tichi notes the manufactured items—spigot, drainboard and rubber sandals—arguing that the "edges are sharp; each component is distinctly profiled, from the grooved drain-board to the glass filled with crisping parsley, and the poet himself is redefined. The designer has supplanted the romantic singer." She goes on to say, "Williams was realizing how to apply his medical education to poetry,"[14] referring to his diagnostic eye, which registers sharp detail. What needs to be added to her reading is Williams's participation in the sanitation movement. The clean, grooved porcelain sink is a modern American product—part of the beginnings of modern kitchen design that will include continuous countertops, integrated sinks, and (in the 1930s) tabletop electric ranges.[15] This 1917 poem expresses awareness of the importance of a "spotless floor" and a well-ordered kitchen—not just because cleanliness is virtuous, but because, as the Charlotte surgical advertisement shows, sanitation is scientific.

Nevertheless, as he showed in "Night in June," Williams was ambivalent about the scientifically defined need for cleanliness, an ambivalence that shows in "Le Médicin Malgré Lui." There a physician complains that he should

> wash the walls of my office
> polish the rust from
> my instruments and keep them
> definitely in order
>
> (*CPi* 122)

This is the lament of the unsuccessful physician whose instruments are unclean from lack of use, whose medical journals are unread, and whose examining room is not sterile. In other words, his lack of success can be attributed to inefficiency stemming from lack of order.

Williams goes on to parody American formulas for success by extending the idea of cleanliness and order involved in a safe, modern medical practice to personal grooming. This doctor could add to his sterile surgery and well-organized medical reference texts "a bill at the tailor's / and at the cleaners" and might even grow "a decent beard" and cultivate "a look / of importance" (*CPi* 122). These changes will enable him to be "a credit to [his] Lady Happiness / and never think anything / but a white thought!" Clearly Williams is spoofing the medical establishment. Many of his texts take jabs at his fellow practitioners, particularly the Rome journal and *A Voyage to Pagany,* but his choice of images in this poem is telling. He moves from problems specific to medical sanitation, through strategies for success, to "white" thinking— thought that is so clean, it is clear. Often in Williams's texts these two principles—accurate vocabulary and extreme cleanliness— appear together.[16]

As Ludwik Fleck has argued, disease does not exist without language. There is organic dysfunction, but a disease as a definable, clearly represented entity must have a name that has (and is) currency within the grammar of the medical discourse. Williams's desire for clear presentation or fresh naming is most evident when he discusses cleanliness: "Clean, clean he had taken each word and made it new for himself so that at last it was new, free from the world for himself" (*I* 167). Those words are ideal because with them one can depict a free, uncontaminated world, create a poem that is object in itself and that serves as a repetition of the "natural" object. His famous "Red Wheelbarrow" is a poem and therefore an object (the primary tenet of Objectivism). The red wheelbarrow, which is cold and wet to the touch, stands in a repetitious relation to the poem through the immediacy of clean words and a clinically pure gaze. It is a physical manifestation or a natural inscription that can be re-presented with a clean, precise vocabulary. "The Red Wheelbarrow" is "contaminated" by the ambiguous reference "So much depends," yet it is, from the medical perspective, the result of *une prise d'être*.

In the early poem "Rain," Williams's typographical technique (a forerunner of his later triadic line) can be seen as an attempt to produce clean words. By spacing out his words separately, he keeps them isolated on the page, almost emptied of contextual meaning. With virtually no punctuation, syntax is difficult to determine. The enjambed lines make each separate word "stand crystal clear with no attachments" (*SE* 128). Stephen Cushman describes the phenomenon: "This grouping of successive elements (words) and events (lineations) becomes the basis of prosody in non-metrical verse. This prosody is neither temporal nor accentual. For lack of a more precise terminology I will call it 'phenomenological.' Enjambing lineation cuts a word off from its immediate contexts and holds it up for inspection, highlighting it among its neighbors."[17] With his newly cleansed words, the poet takes up the details of his and his wife's life together. Objects inside and outside the house are picked up and examined, just as the reader takes up and examines each word, and the poem comes

> perfectly
> into form from its
>   liquid
>
> clearness
>   (*CP1* 346)

In a sense the typography itself, trickling over the page, cleanses and clarifies. Like medical science, which according to Flexner "must be considered as simply the severest effort capable of being made in the direction of purifying, extending, and organizing knowledge,"[18] Williams's attitude toward the words he uses in his poetry is of the same severity.

The problems inherent in this notion of language emerge in his various discussions of Marianne Moore. In his 1931 essay on her work he writes:

> Miss Moore gets great pleasure from wiping soiled words or cutting them clean out, removing the aureoles that have been pasted about them or taking them bodily from greasy contexts. For the compositions which Miss Moore intends, each word should first stand crystal clear with no attachments; not even an aroma. As a cross light upon this, Miss Moore's personal dislike for flowers that have both a satisfying appearance and an odor of perfume is worth noticing. With Miss Moore a word is a word most when it is separated out by science, treated with acid to remove the smudges, washed, dried and placed right side up on a clean surface. Now one may say that this is a word. Now it may be used, and how?
>
> It may be used not to smear it again with thinking (the attachments of thought) but in such a way that it will remain scrupulously itself, clean perfect, unnicked beside other words in parade. (*SE* 128–29)

This passage can be read as part of his lingering allegiance to imagism or Pound's luminous moments and as another of his diatribes against a stale tradition—"greasy contexts." Also characteristic is his move away from excessive erudition and an emphasis on the details of one's locality—typically the sight and smell of flowers.[19] But it is also important to read this essay in relation to Williams's specific circumstances. Words, like his poor Rutherford and Passaic patients, are in greasy and strangely fragrant circumstances, and even when cleaned there lingers the potential for regriming. The doctor/chemist is at work cleaning the words (his tools) to a sterile brightness with acid and arranging them neatly on a clean surface, on the sterile shelves of his surgery. There they remain detailed, separated, identifiable, and unnicked under the free clinical gaze—the gaze that is the "acme point of white penetration" (*SE* 122).

In the preface to *Kora in Hell* Williams quotes Moore: "My work has come to have just one quality of value in it: I will not touch or have to do with those things which I detest" (*I* 10). She follows one of Williams's pronouncements—keep it clean—but violates another—contact. Similar to the Puritans Williams damned in *In the American Grain,* Moore refuses to touch the "Indians";

hence, she in part denies the local. The same problem is evident in medical practice in general. Doctors are acutely aware of the necessity of sanitation for the prevention of disease and for hastening recovery. They know (often) what causes infection, and therefore work for cleanliness, yet at the same time they are the ones (along with the poor and sick) who are most often exposed to filth and disease—a point tied closely to the invention of many medical technologies. One of the reasons Laënnec's stethoscope did not catch on immediately was that his was a short wooden tube that necessarily brought the physician into close physical contact with the patient. The relationship of technology to physician contact remains problematic. In 1931 James Herrick asked, "Should we no longer feel for an enlarged spleen, a presystolic thrill? Are we to give up the attempt to locate by percussion an infiltrated area in the lung or fluid in the pleural cavity? Are we to discard the stethoscope and cardiac murmurs and bronchial breathing and rely on the X-ray and electrocardiograph?"[20]

Nevertheless, medicine demands that the most filthy, diseased parts be examined, brought in close intimacy to the eyes, ears, nose, and hands. The doctor cannot have both cleanliness and contact simultaneously, a point Williams's poem "Marianne Moore" raises:

> Will not some dozen sacks of rags
> observant of intelligence
> conspire from their outlandish cellar
> to evade the law?
>
> Let them, stuffed up, appear
> before her door at ten some night
> and say : Marianne, save us!
> Put us in a book of yours.
>
> Then she would ask the fellow in
> and give him cake
> and warm him with her talk
> before he must return to the dark street.
> (*CP1* 129–30)

Given his frequently expressed admiration for Moore, the poem strikes an odd note. On the one hand, she does let the ragman in and feeds him—touches him (more or less)—but on the other hand, finally it seems doubtful she will save him (clean him) by putting him in a book. She is more likely to put him back in the street, which she does (after letting him eat cake). The poem shows the disparity between cleanliness and contact and, on a political level, the reactionary nature of the desire for that kind of cleanliness. It also dramatizes Williams's own technological position—the included/excluded physician. Unlike Moore, Williams gets dressed and goes out to visit the sacks of rags in their outlandish cellars who share with him a bottle of beer or a lusty moment. Even if he cannot actually cure and cleanse them, he does put them in his books.

Obviously words cannot be cleansed in the same way as surgical instruments, and the idea of a transparent vocabulary (what Roland Barthes tellingly calls "white writing") is a chimera—a problem Williams confronted professionally and poetically. His review of Pound's *A Draft of XXX Cantos* begins with some commonplace observations about particular cantos and then moves to a discussion of Pound's use of words: "A criticism of Pound's *Cantos* could not be better concerned, I think, than in considering them in relation to the principal move in imaginative writing today—that away from the word as a symbol toward the word as reality" (*SE* 107). Related to Williams's own work (and to his endorsement of objectivism), the comment is problematic. Unlike Gertrude Stein, whose words, ripped from any syntactic meaning, seem to become things-in-themselves (e.g., *Tender Buttons*),[21] Williams's own poetic nearly always relies on a referential reality. Although he was sympathetic to and at times exploited the modernist impulse to fetishize words as signifiers divorced from signifieds, more often he tried to make the connection between words and things as explicit as possible; hence his detailed descriptions of everyday objects.[22] "The Rain" might space the words out and reduce their aroma, but, on the whole, their referents remain relatively unproblematic.

He goes on to say that Pound's work "stands out from almost all other verse by a faceted quality that is not muzzy, painty, wet. It is a dry, clean use of words. Yet look at the words. They are themselves not dead. They have not been violated by 'thinking.' They have been used willingly by thought" (*SE* 111). Here Williams's ideal clearly points toward cleansing words of their accumulated filth—traditional poetic associations—but not their direct, instrumental meaning. From a medical perspective, the immediacy of the factual world and the necessity for an (approaching) accurate vocabulary denies the paralysis of phenomenological musing. The physician may doubt his descriptive powers, but he must act as if he did not. Williams's solution for the cleanliness/contact paradox is another form of localism. His words can be clean without emptying their meaning; they can have an aroma if it is fresh. This reconciliation is expressed in *The Embodiment of Knowledge,* where he praises Shakespeare: "Therefore he writes, attempting to strike straight to the core of his inner self, by words. By words which have been used time without end by other men for the same purpose, words worn smooth, greasy with the thumbing and fingering of others. For him they must be fresh too, fresh as anything he knows—as fresh as morning light, repeated every day the year around" (*EK* 105). Unlike his discussion of Moore, Williams here recognizes that all words are smudged and, regardless of modern sanitation technologies, cannot be cleansed. Words are contagious, and like medical technologies, they produce as well as diagnose disease. He respects them as objects, bodies (perhaps diseased) that have been touched before and are going to be touched again.

Williams can desire clean words—white thoughts, white writing—and the medical profession can hold them up as a scientific ideal, but finally their cleanliness is a mirage: "I touch words and they baffle me. I turn them over in my mind and look at them but they mean little that is clean. They are plastered with muck out of the cities" (*I* 175). As a physician and a poet, he needs to confront directly the phenomenal world unimpeded by a blinding tradition, but in both professions he must begin in the muck, enjoy it, and ultimately remain there. Regardless of modern innovations, we cannot live in a sterile world: "A cat licking herself solves most of the problems of infection. We wash too much and finally it kills us" (*I* 258).

CHAPTER 7

Public Health, Plague, and Apocalypse

Bad art is then that which does not serve in the continual service of cleansing the language of all fixations upon dead, stinking dead, usages of the past. Sanitation and hygiene or sanitation that we may have hygienic writing.
—*Letter to Robert Creeley*

Although epistemologies have varied over time, they have always been war machines defending science against its enemies—first in the good old days against religion, then against some of the illusions generated by too much optimism in science itself, still later against the dangers that totalitarian states represent for the autonomy of free scientific inquiry, and finally against the abuse of science distorted by politicians or corporate interests. These polemical versions of what science is and should be are convenient to fight the barbarians and keep them at arms length; they are of no avail for describing what a polemic is and how science and war have come to be so intermingled.
—*Bruno Latour*

However hopeless it may seem, we have no other choice: we must go back to the beginning; it must all be done over; everything that is must be destroyed.
—In the American Grain

Paul Erlich's 1909 discovery of Salvarsan—an effective treatment for syphilis—was hailed as the "magic bullet." As implied by the military metaphor, it was a chemical compound that could locate the cause of infection in a patient's body and destroy it. This medical epistemology (based on germ theory), when turned toward the population at large, constitutes humans as objects in need of aggressive protection from infective agents. The broader role of medicine in preventing disease, as well as in controlling a potentially unruly and immoral populace, has a long history in medical practice. The job of the public health official is to maintain a healthy populace by locating the cause of infection and eliminating it. In the "body politic," these infective agents are often the sick poor and their environs. The public health gaze sees those statistically at risk for disease (either contracting or transmitting) as members of a different population—the "other" who for various failings (hygienic and moral) bring disease on themselves and threaten the health and well-being of the rest of the populace. As the reformer Robert Hartley claimed in 1854, "*social demoralization and crime,* as well as disease, originate and thrive amidst the festering corruptions and pollutions of the miserable accommodations afforded the poor. There is something so congenial in their nature, that 'dirt, disease and crime are concurrent.' "[1]

Concern for the sick poor has a long history in medicine, dating back at least to earlier versions of the Hippocratic oath, which demanded a doctor who "cures without a fee and succors the poor" (a line dropped by the present medical establishment). That concern, while aligned with altruism and related to the medicine's precapitalist economic formation, becomes problematic as the medical profession gains legal power in the community through the institutionalization of the physician's role in public health issues. In the early part of this century, Howard Kelly, a leading gynecologist, observed: "The personal services of the poor must daily invade our doors and penetrate every nook in our houses; if we care for them in no wise beyond their mere service, woe betide us. Think of these countless currents flowing daily in our cities from the houses of the poorest into those of the richest, and forming a sort of civic circulatory system expressive of the life of the body politic, a circulation which continually tends to equalize the distribution of morality and disease."[2] Kelly's circulatory metaphor shows how readily a physician can move from a conception of infection specific to the human body to one of society at large. His concern is directed toward disease's ability to break down social hierarchies at the same time it breaks down individual people's health. The point where modern medicine treats units larger than individual bodies—public health—involves a conceptual leap from the single human to aggregates and often carries with it potentially confusing metaphors.

A crucial theme in the discourse of public health is the material context in which disease occurs. Bernadino Ramazzini, whose *Diseases of Workers* (1713) was one of the first modern "public health" documents, emphasizes the doctor's awareness of employment-related illness: "For so runs the oracle of our inspired teacher: 'When you come to a patient's house, you should ask him what sort of pains he has, what caused them, how many days he has been ill, whether the bowels are working and what sort of food he eats.' So says Hippocrates in his work *Affections.* I may venture to add one more question: What occupation does he follow?"[3] Ramazzini raises what to twentieth-century readers is a commonplace (particularly in popular medicine): employment-related illness is endemic in industrial societies. What is often left out of such comments (or remains implicit) is that the poor are the ones working in those dangerous sites.[4] Although Ramazzini does discuss some guilds, much of his study is devoted to the illnesses of blacksmiths, tinsmiths, stonecutters, corpse bearers, and cleaners of privies and cesspits—in other words, the lower classes.

One of the most influential western public health documents, the title of which points to the class distinctions involved, is Edwin Chadwick's *Report on the Sanitary Condition of the Labouring Population of Great Britain* (1842). Chadwick's report is primarily a compilation of eyewitness accounts by medical officers who visited the homes and neighborhoods of the working classes, and many bear remarkable resemblance to some of Williams's texts. In these narratives, the medical officer, like his imperialist counterparts in India and Africa, moves into an alien territory completely different from and somewhat frightening to middle class mores: "[In the parish of Colerne] the filth, the dilapidated buildings, the squalid appearance of the majority of the lower orders, have a sickening effect upon the stranger who first visits this place. During three years' attendance on the poor of this district, I have never known the small-pox, scarlatina, or the typhus fever to be absent. The situation is damp, and the buildings unhealthy, and the inhabitants themselves inclined to be of dirty habits."[5] The sickening effect is, on the whole, accompanied by a fear of these alien people and a desire to enforce proper behavior: "I am quite sure if such persons were placed in good, comfortable, clean cottages, the improvement in themselves and children would soon be visible, and the exceptions would only be found in a few of the poorest and most wretched, who perhaps had been born in a mud hovel, and had lived in one the first 30 years of their lives."[6]

A recurring image in the Chadwick report is the implied comparison of the poor to animals, which furthers their construction as the "other": "There is commonly only one receptacle for refuse in a court of eight, ten or twelve densely crowded houses. In the year 1836–7, I attended a family of 13, twelve of whom had typhus fever, without a bed in the *cellar,* without straw or timber shavings—frequent substitutes. They lay on the floor, and so crowded, that I could scarcely pass between them."[7] At times, the comparison is more explicit: "We learned that a considerable part of the rent of the houses was paid by the produce of the dungheaps. Thus, worse off than wild animals, many of which withdraw to a distance and conceal their ordure, the dwellers in these courts had converted their shame into a kind of money by which their lodging was to be paid."[8] Chadwick and the sanitary reform movement that grew out of his report were concerned with the health of the labouring classes, but the text also has a voyeuristic quality very much involved in the staging of the poor as objects of curiosity, ridiculing their slovenly habits, and constituting them as animals or children who must suffer the moral uplifting administered by the enlightened middle classes.

In the United States, this middle-class voyeurism can be seen in the texts of Dorothea Dix, the famous reformer of insane asylums. In her "Memorial to the Legislature of Massachusetts" (1843) she writes: "I shall be obliged to speak with great plainness, and to reveal many things revolting to the taste, and from which my woman's nature shrinks with peculiar sensitiveness. But truth is the highest consideration. *I tell what I have seen*—painful and shocking as the details often are."[9] What she has seen are "Insane Persons confined within this Commonwealth, in *cages, closets, cellars, stalls, pens! Chained, naked, beaten with rods,* and *lashed* into obedience!"[10] She describes in Sudbury: "In a stall, built under a woodshed on the road, was a naked man, defiled with filth, furiously tossing through the bars and about the cage, portions of a straw (the only furnishing of his prison) already trampled to chaff."[11] The primary rhetorical strategy in Dix's texts is her insistence on seeing everything with her own eyes. Often the proprietors of the almshouses or the prisons did not want to admit her into some of the cells or stalls, offering various excuses, including the need to protect her femininity, but she would always insist and faithfully report what she had seen: "I requested to see her, but was answered that she 'wasn't fit to be seen; she was naked, and made so much trouble they did not know how to get along.' I hesitated but a moment; I must see her, I said. I cannot adopt descriptions of the condition of the insane secondarily; what I assert for fact, I must see for myself."[12] Reformers depend heavily on the rhetoric of enlightenment—their ability to penetrate to the heart of the scene and expose to all the sordid details of unenlightened practices.

The paternalism of the medical profession toward the sick poor is perhaps most clearly manifested in the hospitals, which in the nineteenth century were primarily charity institutions for the "deserving" poor and were used, at least in part, as a means of social control. They helped keep the poor at work rather than losing time being sick (or infecting others), but perhaps more important, hospitals helped monitor their moral state,[13] as the 1861 regulations for Massachusetts General Hospital show: "The patients are expected to be quiet and exemplary in their behavior, and to conform strictly to the rules and regulations of the Trustees and the orders and prescriptions of the various officers in the establishment; and no indecent or immoral conduct in any patient or other person connected with or resident in the Hospital, shall be tolerated by the Resident Physician, who shall forthwith report any such misconduct to the Visiting Committee."[14] Much of the discourse of public health centers on a concern for the situation of the sick and possibly infectious poor and, at the same time, on their segregation in slums, public housing, or hospitals. There doctors or public health workers are admitted in order to report back to the public at large, and the institutional power of the medicalized state can enforce proper moral behavior.

In the twentieth century, concern focused not simply on moral management but also on economic efficiency. Reformers adopted many of the same machine metaphors discussed in chapter 5 and, as a consequence, reduced the sick to the equivalent of interchangeable parts. Thomas Parran in a 1929 speech on the virtual epidemic of venereal disease observes: "This is the day of intensive organization, of specialization, of expert talent, of complicated machinery; and most industrial plants see to it that their machinery is constantly inspected and kept in the very best running order. But all too many of us rely on the natural course of events as regards the most important element in the success of that business, namely, the human machine."[15] Parran, who later led

the Public Health Service's war on venereal disease, uses economic rhetoric to advocate aggressive treatment of the populace.
Le Corbusier, whose solution to the social problems of the modern era is architecture ("machines for living"), sees the actual
housing of his day as pathological: "The machine that we live in is
an old coach full of tuberculosis."[16] Twentieth-century public
health officials' concern for the poor ranges from altruism to moral
management,[17] economic necessity, smug paternalism and out-
and-out racism.[18]

Many of Williams's texts resemble Chadwick's report and are,
in a sense, the result of a "public health" epistemology. The "case"
of Doloros Marie Pischak (one of the improvisations in *The Descent of Winter*) is a classic example: "Born, September 15, 1927,
2nd child, wt. 6 lbs. 2 ozs. The hero is Dolores Marie Pischak,
the place Fairfield, in my own state, my own country, its largest
city, my own time" (*I* 241). Like Chadwick's agents, he notes
specific details, no matter how insignificant. Although he peri-
odically launches into an improvisational discussion of "decency"
or charismatic men ("A man who might be general or president of
a corporation, or president of the states. Runs a bootleg saloon.
Great!" [*I* 242–43]), he always comes back to the specific details
of his visit into this unknown territory. Loosely framed as a quest
narrative (the Doctor is looking for Pischak's house), the text is a
minute description of "Fairfield," and the reader is allowed to see
what seems to be the entire town in every bit of its filth, squalor,
and beauty: "Here a goose flaps his wings by a fence, a white
goose, women talk from second story windows to a neighbor on
the ground, the tops of the straggling backyard poplars have been
left with a tail of twigs and on the bare trunk a pulley with a line in
it is tied. A cop whizzes by on his sidecar cycle, the bank to the
river is cinders where dry leaves drift. The cinders are eating
forward over the green grass below, closer and closer to the river
bank, children are in the gutters violently at play over a dam of
mud, old women with seamed faces lean on the crooked front
gates" (*I* 241). He does, it appears, eventually locate and deliver
the baby mentioned in the opening section, but the focus of this
improvisation, like many public health texts, is the journey into
the heart of darkness and the detailing of the conditions that exist
there.[19] Unlike public health texts, Williams's is virtually free of
overt moralism, substituting instead his overwhelming enthusi-

asm for the sight, sounds, and smells he encounters in his trip to see how the "others" live.

Williams's journeys into this unknown world usually contain a sense of wonder, exhilaration, but still he maintains his isolation. The tawdry becomes beautiful, the pathetic heroic, and the doctor achieves a level of contact. These texts are occasioned by the medical but rarely about it. The early poem "Sick African" takes place in the house of a black couple:

> Wm. Yates, colored,
> Lies in bed reading
> The Bible—
> And recovering from
> A dose of epididymitis
> Contracted while Grace
> Was pregnant with
> The twelve day old
> Baby:
> There sits Grace, laughing,
> Too weak to stand.
>
> (*CP1* 59)

Presumably the narrator has come to check on the baby and treat the husband for a genital infection, but clearly his delight is in detailing the scene. In *Principles and Practice of Medicine,* Osler notes that epididymitis can occur in secondary-stage syphilis,[20] but because of the limited passage of time in the poem, that diagnosis is unlikely. Although the Wasserman test was developed in 1906, in 1917 doctors had no readily available test for gonorrhea, so diagnoses of genito-urinary infections were not always precise. Given the perception among physicians of a higher incidence of venereal disease among blacks, "The Sick African" surely implies that William Yates was not monogamous during his wife's pregnancy—a point that sharpens the incongruity of his Bible reading and his wife's laughing. The poem's poignancy is derived from white middle-class presuppositions about black family life. Here Williams's obvious delight conflicts with the ideal of the moral management of the poor. The doctor as representative of middle-class morality should censure, not delight in, such behavior. Nevertheless, in its own jocular way, the poem displays the "other" as an object of curiosity.

Williams also used the strategies of the surrealists (and a touch of racism) to emphasize the alien nature of the slums. "The Jungle" opens in "the / breathless interior of the wood, / tangled with wrist-thick // vines, the flies, reptiles, / the forever fearful monkeys / screaming and running" (*CPI* 241–42). The physician, trained to deal with individual illness, is disoriented by the squalor in which he finds himself. But he locates the house, and "a girl waiting / shy, brown, soft-eyed— / to guide you / Upstairs, sir" (*CPI* 242). The constitution of the sick poor as "other," coupled with the disorientation produced by their alien world provokes a surreal, almost demonic response in *Kora in Hell:* "He plunges up the dark steps on his grotesque deed of mercy. In his warped brain an owl of irony fixes on the immediate object of his care as if it were the thing to be destroyed, guffaws at the impossibility of putting any kind of value on the object inside or of even reversing or making less by any other means than induced sleep—which is no solution—the methodical gripe of the sufferer. Stupidity couched in a dingy room beside the kitchen. One room stove-hot, the next the dead cold of a butcher's ice box. The man leaned and cut the baby from its stem. Slop in disinfectant, roar with derision at the insipid blood stench" (*I* 65–66). These poor patients no longer delight; they simply disgust, and they are assaulted in the guise of care. The very details of the house are pathological, so the doctor slops in the disinfectant desiring to sanitize the entire contaminated field.

Historically, physicians have demonstrated concern for establishing and maintaining their authority in the eyes of the general public in order to treat individual patients effectively. They can also gain authority through alignment with various public health bureaucracies—a strategy of increasing significance in the twentieth century. Because of the structure of modern medicine (ease of transportation and communication), patients have the option and are encouraged to seek a second opinion (even though the AMA rigorously regulates the behavior of consulting physicians). Consequently, in order to assert their own particular view of health (and its attendant morality), physicians find it necessary to align themselves with other state structures. Mansfield Merriman, discussing sanitary science, draws the following distinction: "Hygiene is the preservation of the health of the individual under the rules of the physician, while sanitary science has for its aim the preservation and protection of the health of the community under the combined action of physicians, engineers, and the civil authorities."[21] When medicine becomes connected to the state, the doctor wields a power different from that of a trusted family friend. He can fail a patient's physical and therefore keep him or her from working, attending school, or getting insurance. Conversely, he can exempt someone from work or military service, advocate a disability pension, or excuse a crime.[22]

Duties in bureaucratic medical positions, though often *pro bono,* are also used to develop and expand private practice. Williams's son William Eric notes that his father provided free medical care to the children at the county orphanage in Hackensack early in his career to develop his reputation.[23] He also served on the Bergen County mosquito commission and was a school physician for fourteen years.[24] His poem "The Poor" details his experience as a school physician:

> By constantly tormenting them
> with reminders of the lice in
> their children's hair, the
> School Physician first
> brought their hatred down on him.
> But by this familiarity
> they grew used to him, and so,
> at last,
> took him for their friend and adviser.
>
> (*CP1* 159)

A school physician can be a constant torment to the poor, and they can do little about it since he is appointed by the school board. The poem is a parable of medicine in a modern economy. The doctor uses whatever means at his disposal to expand his practice—from the schoolchildren to their families and neighbors—and thus consolidates his position within the community. Although the narrator of "The Poor" claims them as his friends, he distances himself through a class distinction—the poor with their attendant maladies, "lice"—and the last word of the poem is not "friend" but "adviser." He has won the trust of the poor not in order to be accepted but instead to change their lives according to the prevailing health standards. This is not to imply that Williams was in some way craven or mercenary in his development and maintenance of his practice. Indeed, all evidence points to the opposite conclusion. Nevertheless, the prevailing attitude of many public health reformers is decidedly evangelical. They have the key to the health of the social body, and the point of contact is necessarily the vigorous management of the diseased—here the poor who drain off the energies of a healthy social system.

Because they are constituted as "other," the poor, like their microbial counterparts, are subject to a degree of experimentation or exploitation. The most grievous example of such exploitation is the famous Tuskegee syphilis study begun by the Public Health Service in 1934 and not concluded until 1974. Four hundred black farmers were infected with the syphilis spirochete and left untreated in order to trace the symptoms over the life of the disease.[25] Williams, in his public health role, never participated in anything so obscene. Rather, his use of the poor as objects appears in his imaginative writing. The best evidence of this is his "red notebook," a small book he used while working as a school physician in 1914.[26] There, interspersed between notes listing cases of mumps and chicken pox, are fragments of speech, "I ain't had a bath for 4 weeks dirt eatin' me up—setting up here bad to be so poor" (13), and observations: "I see for a moment how everything is dependent on the curve of one of the children's legs—as art— that is the fundamental manifestation of life" (6). These latter phrases suggest art (the echoing lines of many abstract paintings), a medical concern (for proper skeletal development and treatment of rickets), the opening of his famous "Red Wheelbarrow" poem, and his own oddly sexual depiction of children (a point reinforced by a later observation: "I bless the muscles of their legs, their necks that are limber, their hair that is like new grass, their eyes that are not always dancing their postures so naive and graceful, their voices that are full of fright & other passions their transparent shams & their mimicry of adults—the softness of their bodies—" (26)).[27] These are typical of Williams's poetic, professional, and personal concerns, yet given the context of their appearance—a notebook carried by the school physician—they point toward a manifestation of a "public health" attitude. These children are objects of medical and social concern, but they are also clearly an embodiment of the "other," a group that needs uplifting: "Rosa Robitza Washington—Sent home for uncleanliness" (7). To echo his poem "Marianne Moore," they need to be cleaned and put in a book.

The duties of a doctor as a physician and as a public admin-istrator intersect during catastrophic epidemics, a theme frequently explored in literature and one that shows up in several of Williams's texts. An early Western description of a devastating plague, Thu-cydides' "Pestilence at Athens," emphasizes the physician's in-ability to curb the epidemic: "For not only were physicians unable to do anything at first, owing to the ignorance with which they carried out treatment, but they themselves died in greatest num-bers for the very reason that they came most in contact with the cases."[28] The physicians were ineffective, and they also lost the isolation that separated them from the sick. Epidemics confirm Howard Kelly's worst fears; they are democratic. Only through great effort can social distinctions (and the various economies that rely on segregation and flows) be maintained. In Thucydides, the breakdown of the body by disease is paralleled by a breakdown of social and moral hierarchies. The victims "became negligent of things sacred and profane alike. . . . For people more readily dared to indulge in sexual pleasures which they had previously concealed, seeing the sudden change in fortunes of rich men who died suddenly. . . . Consequently, men saw fit to gratify their fleeting lusts and to make pleasure their chief aim."[29] Most illness strikes rich and poor indiscriminately (though today's demogra-phers demonstrate otherwise). As Williams comments in *Kora in Hell:* "After some years of varied experience with the bodies of the rich and the poor a man finds little to distinguish between them, bulks them as one and bases his working judgments on other matters" (*I* 46). But plague, which seems to universalize death, tightens the focus on disease's leveling capacity. The plague of Athens erased social distinctions and at the same time produced a macabre carnival—a chaos that subverts all social distinction.

Inspired by successes such as Walter Reed's, public health offi-cials in the early part of the twentieth century desired to eradicate all infectious diseases. In order to do so, they needed to establish a crisis mentality in the general populace, which would then grant them the authority necessary for large sanitary projects; conse-quently, their texts often employed a plague rhetoric.[30] Indeed, a rhetoric of crisis pervades the very concept of twentieth-century public health. Mansfield Merriman defines the problems of sani-tary engineers in these terms: "It therefore appears that health should not be regarded as the normal state of man under natural conditions, but rather as an ideal state which might occur under ideal conditions. Disease, in strictness, is to be regarded as the normal state and health as the state insured by eternal vigilance in removing the causes that continually tend to produce disease and death."[31] The effect of this model of health is the granting of broad powers to public health officials. If health occurs only in ideal circumstances, life in the "natural" world must be conducted as life in a plague.

In literary accounts of plagues as diverse as Daniel Defoe's *Journal of the Plague Year* and Albert Camus's *La peste,* the physicians usually maintain their social authority even in the face of their inability to curb the epidemic. Nevertheless, their authority does them precious little good if they are the ones most exposed to the disease. In "The Plague in Myth and Literature," René Girard briefly surveys Western representations of plagues, arriving at this conclusion: "The plague is universally presented as a process of undifferentiation, a destruction of specificities."[32] Most plague texts demonstrate an overwhelming fear of the anarchy brought on by the erasure of difference, but at the same time, depict the use of those fears to reestablish hierarchy. It is the doctor's role as both a physician and a representative of the public good (middle-class values) to curb both plagues—to heal the sick and maintain economic and social structures.[33] If the role of the physician is taken into account, however, Girard's notion of universal leveling breaks down. The doctors do experience the frenzy of epidemic disease and its attendant social disruption, and they do become susceptible to the disease they are trying to treat, but they also are important markers of social authority and, on the whole, demand respect and command authority.

Though not as devastating as the 1918 pandemic, the East Coast influenza epidemic of 1929 was a medical nightmare. Williams's notebook, revised and later published as "January" in *A Novelette and Other Prose,* is not a typical "plague" journal. It bears stronger resemblance to *Kora in Hell* and the prose sections of *Spring and All* and "Descent of Winter" than to descriptions of quarantines and administrative measures. Nevertheless, his style creates an intensity of the moment, and in that intensity he manifests a "plague mentality." Thucydides records the Athenian debate on whether the oracle had predicted a war and a famine or a war and a plague, but for Williams both hunger and an epidemic intensify experience. After a remarkably detailed description of a cat, some birds, and the marks left by a raindrop, Williams relates the epidemic to hunger. Americans, who are never hungry, do not appreciate food the same way as the French, who have experienced want: "It is because the stresses of life have sharpened the sight. Life is keener, more pressed for place—as in an epidemic. . . . It is that a stress pares off the inanity by force of speed and a sharpness, a closeness of observation, of attention comes through" (*I* 273). The key points here for Williams, one relating him to older plague narratives and one to the emergent modern world, are "sharpness" and "speed." "January" is a text of sharp detail and quick breaks from one idea or conversation to another. The narrator moves fast—both physically (in his car) and intellectually (his mind shifts between banal conversations, quick diagnoses, romantic liaisons, and intense observations of specific details). That shifting makes problematic the relation between what Girard calls the "erasure of difference"[34] and Williams's increased sharpness of vision, which, by focusing on specific details, creates a new or different hierarchy.

Throughout "January" Williams comments on his own heightened senses, at times in contexts such as the discussion of France above, but often through his own performance: "Where the drop of rain had been, there remained a delicate black stain, the outline of the drop marked clearly on the white paint, in black, within which a shadow, a smoothest tone faded upward between the lines and burst them, thinning out upon the woodwork down which the rain had come. In the tops of the screws the polishing powder could be seen white" (*I* 273). Apart from what could be seen as a physician's obsession with cleanliness—black stains on white paint and the scouring powder in the screws—this passage's clarity of observation is heightened by its position in a text concerned with life, death, speed, and sex. The hierarchy of diagnostic vision is asserted because the narrative does stop, just for a moment, to observe the delicate tracings of a raindrop.

Williams's wife[35] becomes the object the epidemic allows him to see: "Imagine then that I see you in such a light. Imagine then why I cling to you. It is a fierce singleness that the epidemic has stepped up to a mountain. Imagine then why I have—why it has been impossible for me to think of not being married" (*I* 294). The irony of this passage is that his vision is not directed exclusively at Floss, but instead at many women: "That singleness I see in everything—actual—which has been my life, because of the haste due to the epidemic, I see in you and so you become beautiful partly because you are so but partly because of other women" (*I* 283). Because "January" lacks a coherent narrative thread, it is impossible to determine the speakers in the many conversations that occur throughout the text, but it is clear that the woman's voice is not always his wife. The inclusion of other women's voices calls attention to the leveling phenomenon of the plague—all women are equally beautiful—as well as its isolating qualities. Death draws a community together (along with the doctor attending), but fear of contagion keeps them apart. The doctor enters the house of disease to provide comfort but must be careful not to touch anything.

In the midst of this social upheaval, Williams creates hierarchies of vision. Like a good diagnostician, he must sort out the objects and focus only on those that have "pathological" significance. Yet at the same time he allows in multiple voices with no clear sense of context or value. As a result, the reader cannot privilege the language of the street ("Not pea NUT, pe CAN" [*I* 274]) over the narrator's discourses on science, philosophy, and art. In the same way, the reader cannot distinguish between the women who are drawn out by the narrator's singular focus. The text takes on at times a carnivalesque quality that undercuts the clear authority of a narrative voice. The problem is complicated even more by Williams's discussion of the relation of writing to his life and to the epidemic:

"Why do you write?"
"For relaxation, relief. To have nothing in my head,—to freshen my eye by that till I see, smell, know and can reason and be." (*I* 289)[36]

Though not explicit in this passage, part of his attitude toward writing is the same as his attitude toward the epidemic, which, among other things, has sharpened his senses and, in a rather strange way, has refreshed him: "The rush that simplifies life, complicates it" (*I* 275). But his writing depends on his profession, while his profession gets in the way of his writing: "Keep up your courage. Get through with this awful drive. There's no way out just now—unless you quit entirely—which seems hardly possible for the moment. It will end soon (in a few years) and then you must write day and night." (*I* 279). This is ironic because at the moment he is writing "January," and there is a long tradition of writing oneself out of a plague—writing as prophylaxis or therapy.[37] Writing can reestablish the hierarchies lost in a plague by recording the intensities of sensual experience heightened by the plague's circumstances, but at the same time, Williams in "January" undercuts the authority gained by the "speaking eye" by means of the work's carnivalesque form.

Epidemics subside, life returns to normal, and hierarchies are restored. In Rutherford, "the snow continues to fall. Calls begin to come in from the outside: not professional. The epidemic is over" (*I* 304). The narrator turns to what he ignored during the frenetic time: "There must be five or six letters lying around unanswered from as far back as four weeks ago. Someone wants me to write an article about my view on the conflict between art, science and philosophy" (*I* 304). The text of "January" changes abruptly here—the speed disappears and the reader is given a version of the essay called for by the letter, ending with a celebration of the "actual" that is the result of the impressions attained through the harrowing and intense experience of doctoring during an epidemic.[38]

In public health as well as medicine, disease eradication is often conceptualized by military metaphors.[39] Infectious agents are invasive and must be fought for the health of the social organism. After Pasteur, the concept of spontaneous generation was abandoned by scientists in favor of germ theory—a more effective metaphor—and medicine began to deal with infection in "modern" terms, as Lister's discussion of antiseptic methods for treating wounds demonstrates:

> In conducting the treatment, the first object must be the destruction of any septic germs which may have been introduced into the wounds, either at the moment of the accident or during the time which has since elapsed. This is done by introducing the acid of full strength into all accessible recesses of the wound by means of a piece of rag held in dressing forceps and dipped into the liquid. This I did not venture to do in earlier cases; but experience has shown that the compound which carbolic acid forms with the blood, and also any portion of tissue killed by its caustic action, including even parts of the bone, are disposed of by absorption and organisation, provided they are afterwards kept from decomposing.[40]

In Lister's treatment, germs and some healthy tissue are destroyed, but that action saves the organism and even reestablishes "organisation." Metaphorically, the social hierarchies are reasserted.

Since germ theory, modern medical discourse has become an armed camp. No longer content to treat symptoms and let the carefully monitored disease run its course *(vis medicatrix naturae),* medicine actively tries to build up defensive postures (vaccination) and attack at the root all filth and infection (public health and therapeutics). Today scientists are only beginning to understand the significant role played by "parasites" in biological systems (human and ecological), particularly systems disrupted by overly aggressive sanitary measures. Indeed, the very term *parasite* is troubling, since it depends on a judgment regarding which single organism is more important. And today even the notion of "single organism" has become a problematic category.[41] What can get lost in these metaphors is the distinction between the microbe (or other nonhuman carrier of the disease) and the humans who are infected. When this medical warfare is turned to the public at large, its results can be horrifying. In Williams's writing, this "public health" epistemology results in frequent imaginative apocalypses.[42]

As a physician concerned with health, Williams would perhaps find it difficult to look over the polluted squalor of the industrialized Passaic River and not envision a "surgical strike"—destroying the village in order to save it. In *Spring and All* he does something along those lines:

> Imagine the monster project of the moment: Tomorrow we the people of the United States are going to Europe armed to kill every man, woman and child in the area west of the Carpathian Mountains (also east) sparing none. Imagine the sensation it will cause. First we shall kill them and then they, us. But we are careful to spare the Spanish bulls, the birds, rabbits, small deer and of course—the Russians. For the Russians we shall build a bridge from edge to edge of the Atlantic—having first been at pains to slaughter all Canadians and Mexicans on this side. Then, oh then, the great feature will take place.
>
> Never mind; the great event may not exist, so there is no need to speak further of it. Kill! kill! the English, the Irish, the French, the Germans, the Italians, and the rest: friends or enemies, it makes no difference, kill them all. The bridge is to be blown up when all Russia is upon it. And why?
>
> Because we love them—all. (*I* 90)

Williams presses his notion of love here to an absurd extreme, but from an admittedly warped public health perspective, this "war" is reasonable. If society is sick, the infection must be eliminated. Lister was concerned with the size of the wound when he applied carbolic acid as antiseptic; healthy flesh was destroyed along with the sepsis. In wars, civilians are killed (what was euphemistically called in the Persian Gulf War "collateral damage"). Williams's diagnosis of a world infected by a paralyzing tradition forces his prescription for radical treatment—extermination.

The rejection of a stale tradition and the desire for clean, pure language are therefore tied to a sanitation/apocalyptic vision. In World War II Williams (following the tradition of the futurists) saw something positive: "War releases energy. Energy can be used to transmute and create. Thus war by releasing energy indirectly serves in the creation of values" ("Midas," *RI* 163). The energy he describes in the abstract soon becomes material, but still with the same positive effect: "The doing away with the slum districts of London is an excellent thing. War has begun the demolition of the slum districts in London" (*RI* 167). Given Williams's literary career, this is a troubling assertion. He was devoted to articulating the beauty found in slums similar to those destroyed by the Luftwaffe. As a physician, he literally saved the people living there, and as a poet, he articulated the beauty. Yet in his "Midas" essay, and more pointedly in "An Exultation," he glories in the destruction: "Let the agents / of destruction purify you with bombs, cleanse / you of the profits of your iniquities to the last / agony of relinquishment" (*CP*2 42).

In modern medicine, the eradication of disease has its methods—purification through destruction—and its price—the loss of healthy "tissue." Those schooled in the ideology of cleanliness are prepared to use those methods and pay that price. From that perspective, the appearance of this apocalyptic vision in Williams's work is not surprising, but it does reveal an underlying tension in many of his texts. As a physician or public health worker, he traveled into the slums and touched the infected tissues. He constituted the sick poor as the "other" and brought them back as objects of curiosity. He occasionally succumbed to the extension of the germ metaphor to the imaginative destruction of the human population. Yet all this is only a thread (however significant) in his writing. Just as often he insists on constituting the sick poor not as objects to be cleansed by an overly aggressive, patriarchal institution, but rather as humans with beauty and dignity.

CHAPTER 8

Paterson, Placebos, and Postmodernism

I have found no cure for the sick.
—"The Yellow Flower"

We are left with that pure and random play of signifiers that we call postmodernism, which no longer produces monumental works of the modernist type but ceaselessly reshuffles the fragments of preexistent texts, the building blocks of older cultural and social production, in some new and heightened bricolage: metabooks which cannibalize other books, metatexts which collate bits of other texts—such is the logic of postmodernism in general.
—Fredric Jameson

Let
me out! (Well go!) this rhetoric
is real!
—Paterson

World War II marks a turning point in world politics, the cultural hegemony of science, and the efficacy of medical practitioners. With the advent of sulfonomides and, later, antibiotics and corticosteroids, physicians were able to produce marked therapeutic advances. Rapid developments throughout the century led to the near eradication or control of many devastating diseases, including widespread inoculation in the United States, culminating with Jonas Salk's polio vaccine. Nevertheless, the postwar period was also a time of uncertain attitudes toward scientific and technological breakthroughs. The American populace had experienced the victory of Western democracy and the ascendancy of the United States as the world's scientific and technological powerhouse, but had also witnessed, by means of the newsreels, the wholesale destruction of much of Europe, heard stories of scientific experimentation in the Nazi death camps, and been both thrilled and horrified by the explosion of the atomic bomb.

In 1946 the *New York State Journal of Medicine* published the proceedings of a conference on "The Use of Placebos in Therapy." The discussion has many of the markings of earlier debates about the efficacy of the materia medica but is couched in terms of scientific certainty. Because of recent pharmacological discoveries and the development of the blind test (three groups—one receiving the drug, one receiving a placebo, and one receiving nothing), a reasonable statistical certainty regarding various drugs' effectiveness had been reached. In those tests, the placebo was a way of providing science's highly prized objectivity, but that objectivity was undercut by the "placebo effect." Consequently, there was a move in medicine to both revise the pharmacopeia[1] and study the placebo. As one member of the panel noted, one-sixth to one-third of the *New York Hospital Formulary* could be considered simple placebo.

Ultimately the subject of the conference is a crisis of authority in the medical profession (and, one could add, society as a whole). At a time when therapeutics was becoming remarkably scientific, attention is once again turned to the social authority of the physician to effect cure: "any pill, whether it be sugar or medication, is in part placebo because it is a symbol of the doctor. In his absence the patient needs his support. When he has a little pill box with tablets to take, that is an interpolation of the doctor. He can carry that much of the doctor with him and it is effective. . . . The pill is the symbol of the doctor's unspoken or spoken words, 'I will take care of you.' A whole body of knowledge, experience, and wisdom is epitomized in that little pill for the patient."[2] Although the debate is specifically about the psychotherapeutic value of the placebo and the role of the physician in what could be construed as deception (unless the physician can convince himself that placebos are acceptable or be fooled by results not supported by statistical science), it is in broader terms about the maintenance of the physician's authority and the efficacy of a complex semiology—the pill *represents* the physician, who in turn represents both health and a stable, patriarchal system. Illness is a disturbance in a homeostatic system and requires an infusion of stability from a monolithically secure structure—the medical profession. The placebo effect demonstrates the power of that semiology to restore homeo-stasis, but at the same time, calls into question the scientifically demonstrable effects of "real" chemicals on "real" organisms.

Just as Galen passed off his cure of another physician as some-thing miraculous, the doctors in the 1946 conference are anxious to maintain their authority and complain at the same time that they glory in it. When discussing the suggestablity of patients relative to their intelligence, one panelist asserts:

> I have made it a rule to distrust so-called "intelligent" people, who are eager to be informed about the details of a treatment on the grounds that they are "intelligent" and can be depended upon to cooperate better with a complete understanding. I need only to be perfectly frank with one of these patients and tell him, for example, that we need to guard against digitalis toxicity, that toxicity makes its appearance with a loss of appetite, spots before the eyes, nausea, vomiting, or premature contractions, when I am promptly confronted by all of these symptoms long before enough of the drug has been taken to exert any effect.[3]

Regardless of the placebo's psychotherapeutic value, here is an open discussion of the same medical confidence game that has been going on for years—the authority of the physician can, in and of itself, greatly affect the health of the patient. What is crucial at this particular point in history is that the "con" is being openly discussed and attempts are being made to bring it into the realm of acceptable practice. The existence now of drugs that are effective (which can be demonstrated by "scientific" testing)[4] allows these physicians to confront older drugs that "do not work," and instead of rejecting them out of hand (though some in the conference do advocate that), they attempt to bring them into the fold. In other words, the *simulation* of cure is being validated as reality, while at the same time, the "reality" of the cure is being to shown to participate in a complex network of meaning production. The sign—be it a medical term or a pill of unknown content—is, in medical semiology, reassuring because it is unfathomable. The more arcane, the better.

A further concern voiced by the panelists was that if a physician used impure placebos (those containing vitamins or other poten-tially potent material), he or she could also succumb to the placebo effect: "The pure placebo relieves only the patient. The impure placebo relieves the doctor's symptoms as well as those of the

patient."[5] This concern is part of the scientization of medicine—
that doctors should only prescribe drugs proven by scientific tests,
not those accepted through a tradition—but it also points to the
possibility that the simulation will become "real" for the doctor,
who also occupies a position in a complex and immensely powerful semiological system and consequently can become (or is) an
effect of that system.

The crisis of authority explored by the panelists of the 1946
conference could be seen as a symptom of what has come to be
called the postmodern condition, but the term *postmodern* must
(like the pill or the word *obstruction*) be used with caution, since
its power is derived in part from its impregnability. According to
Fredric Jameson, *"Postmodernism* is not something we can settle
once and for all and then use with a clear conscience. The concept, if there is one, has to come at the end, and not at the beginning, of our discussions of it."[6] Discussing postmodernism in
relation to Williams and medicine raises two related questions: Is
it a stable concept? And is it a useful concept?

The answer to the first is no. At present the best that we can
muster is postmodernisms—traits that seem to be becoming part
of a cultural dominant and that are in some way different from
earlier, more properly modern thought. I do not believe that any
time soon we will be able to add up those traits and create an
algebra of our age, but we can try to examine each in its textual
and material manifestations and in its historical context. That,
then, is the answer to the second question. The term is useful
because it thrusts us back into history—into historical thinking.
Williams is generally regarded as an important modernist writer,
and I have been arguing all along that this modernism is part and
parcel of the scientific century. What emerges from this analysis
is, perhaps not surprisingly but still clearly evident, a patriarchal
sense of authority firmly embedded in the epistemology of the
age. In Williams's work, poetic authority and scientific objectivity
are closely aligned. One general trait (though it has many guises)
of postmodernism is a denial or subversion of authority. There is
the rejection of totality or metanarratives (Lyotard), the "death" of
the author and subjectivity (Barthes and Foucault), world leaders
and wars that are the effects of entertainment technologies (Rea-
gan, Desert Storm), numerous attacks on the various "centrisms"
and our "stable" cultural heritage in the academy, and, perhaps

most significant, the indifference of the general populace (despite yearly jeremiads by back-to-basics conservatives) to these missing "centers."

Paralleling those political and cultural effects are serious debates in the philosophy and sociology of science about the "authority" of objective science—a powerful questioning of the basic foundations of modern (post-Baconian) science that develops resonance by increasingly pressing ecological problems. The word *postmodern* might not have a clear definition and, when applied to Williams's work, might seem to draw too clear distinctions, yet applying it thus is worth the risk because, even though there might not be a rupture or epistemological break, there is a clear shift in emphasis in his post–World War II work that relates to some of the crises in postmodern culture and contemporary science.

Perhaps unwittingly, the placebo conference sets out these issues. In *Simulations* Jean Baudrillard uses a medical example that provides a perspective:

> To dissimulate is to feign not to have what one has. To simulate is to feign to have what one hasn't. One implies a presence, the other an absence. But the matter is more complicated, since to simulate is not simply to feign: "Someone who feigns an illness can simply go to bed and make believe he is ill. Someone who simulates an illness produces in himself some of the symptoms." (Littre) Thus feigning or dissimulating leaves the reality principle intact: the difference is always clear, it is only masked; whereas simulation threatens the difference between "true" and "false", between "real" and "imaginary".[7]

Baudrillard's notion of simulation as replacing reality (or, from another perspective, the construction of reality through simulation) is of prime importance to much of the debate about postmodernism, but the relation of authority to simulation needs sharpening. Although it is tempting to see today's reproductive/representational technologies as making "reality" problematic, it is only because of those technologies (or as Jameson would argue, the nature of multinational capitalism) that we can see and understand simulation as a phenomenon. It is not that we have lost a reality that was once very present. The reality Baudrillard sets in opposition to simulation has never been *there*. Rather it is produced by authority—by systems designed to make some *thing* knowable, articulable, and (often) powerful. What must be explored are the

circumstances necessary to create and exert the authority to enforce a certain reality as "real" (and not simulation). The placebo
effect, like reproduction, causes "something fundamental to vac-
illate,"[8] and that is the separation of reality from fantasy—a determination that depends on clearly articulated cultural authority (an
ideology of clarity and the theater of proof). When that authority
is threatened (as it is in the postmodern period), the response can
be an attempt to restore it on older grounds (as the placebo panelists try by bringing the placebo effect itself into a scientifically
measurable situation) or to *try* to live without the authority or the
stability of a "real" articulable world—the response of many phi-
losophers of postmodernism.

In a slightly more open fashion, the placebo discussion reenacts
the therapeutic debates of the nineteenth century between those
who advocated *vis medicatrix naturae* and those for heroic intervention. The twentieth century is an age of heroic intervention
(particularly in acute cases), and the psychotherapeutic use of
placebos harks back to homeopathy—a practice effectively crushed
in the United States by the AMA. At the heart of heroic intervention is a view of science as the conquest of nature, the unveiling of
her secrets, and the isolation of the controlling molecule (virus,
atom, etc.)—in other words, the discovery of the first cause or
origin. Heroic intervention gave the world polio vaccines, heart
transplants, and the atomic bomb; the passive method seems to
rely too heavily on subjectivity, specificity, and almost infinite
variability (much of the placebo discussion centered on the abilities of certain physicians to be more suggestive to their patients
than others). Hard science prefers "reality" to "illusion" and
builds mechanisms to prove the difference. Its power rests on the
hierarchy of real and imaginary. It is, on one level, absolutely
crucial to maintain the hierarchy of the physician's superior knowledge, wisdom, and experience for placebos to work, but at the
same time the placebo confounds the more crucial category of
reality and illusion; to use Baudrillard's term, it is a simulation.

The contours of modernism are difficult to chart, but what has
emerged from this discussion of Williams and modern science has
been a concern for objectivity (and objectification), clarity, efficiency, and cleanliness. The mechanisms necessary to realize these
ideals place a great deal of mastery and control in the hands of
those in the center of the systems. There was, without doubt, a

utopian impulse to modernism—humankind was to be liberated from the outmoded, the yoke of the past, and so on—but the modern world would be one governed by visionaries. Le Corbusier said, "Where order reigns, well-being begins." In *Toward a New Architecture* he posits his alternative to revolution—architecture—but his architecture is one of control: "A street such as this would be designed by a single architect to obtain unity, grandeur, dignity and economy."[9] His communities are planned, space is carefully policed, and instead of hidden nooks where crime and punishment can occur, the modern architectural space is penetrable—if not by people, then by light and vision.

Originally praised for its openness and machinelike elegance, many have come to see (with the help of Michel Foucault's discussion of Jeremy Bentham's architecture) that the freedom and clarity of vision obtained by modern architecture is, quite possibly, a more insidious method of disciplining the populace than royal authority and secret police. The modern office with its open floor and half-height partitions creates an illusion of space and freedom of movement, but also allows for effective surveillance and control. From that perspective, white-collar space begins to look like the factory floor of Charlie Chaplin's *Modern Times*. While the intention of modern architecture could have been democratization of style and public space, its effect has been a reinscription of authority and new technologies of social control. According to Jameson, "high modernism is thus credited with the destruction of the fabric of the traditional city and its older neighborhood culture (by way of the radical disjunction of the new Utopian high-modernist building from its surrounding context), while the prophetic elitism and authoritarianism of the modern movement are remorselessly identified in the imperious gesture of the charismatic Master."[10] In the arts, the modern period was a period of masters—Stravinsky, Picasso, Joyce—and an age of magisterial pronouncement.[11] The author function was firmly ensconced in the citadel of power, regardless of T.S. Eliot's rather strained notions of "extinction of personality."

In "Toward the Crystal: Art and Science in Williams' Poetic," Diana Collecut Surman makes a convincing argument for the importance of the image of the crystal in Williams's work, relating it specifically to other modern figures and movements and to the parallel developments in physics of relativity theory and quantum mechanics. Much of her discussion supports my contention that the clean and the clear (the crystalline) are implicated in a scientific epistemology as well as Williams's central poetic concerns. The following are lines Surman discovered in Williams's texts:

"Poetry has to do with the crystallization of the imagination" (*I* 140)

"Words are indivisible crystals" (*I* 160)

"the radiant nothing / of crystalline / spring" (*CP1* 252)

"This crystal sphere / upon whose edge I drive" (*CP2* 16)

These and many others show Williams's lingering allegiance to imagism and to a masculine science that "shoots a clarity into the murk" (*VTP* 116). Surman begins her essay with a discussion of Amédée Ozenfant and Charles-Edouard Jeanneret's book on modern painting, which was an attempt to battle the anarchistic impulses of artists such as Tristan Tzara and Marcel Duchamp. They felt modern painting (specifically cubism, which Williams admired) showed "a tendency toward the crystal."[12] This attitude toward painting is significant, since Jeanneret (Le Corbusier) was also one of the most influential architects of the modern period. His work typifies the International style, which produced the crystalline glass boxes that grace the skylines of most American cities.[13]

The image of the crystal remained in Williams's work for the rest of his career, but in *Paterson* there is a shift in emphasis as the "radiant gist" "resists final crystallization" (*P* 109). The crystal is an image of clarity, science, modernism, and authority, but at this point in his career, Williams's attitude toward authority and the relationship between the clearly presented object, the beautiful thing (woman), and the privileged perceiver (penetrator) becomes problematic. There is, in *Paterson* and the late poems, a counterstress—the subversion of authority, patriarchy, and modernism.[14]

The image of the radiant gist is followed by, "There was an earlier day, of prismatic colors : whence / to New Barbados came an Englishman . / Thus it began ." The reference is to Williams's father, who met his mother in the Caribbean; thus Williams's own life began. But the opening line resonates, particularly given its juxtaposition with the radiant gist. First it calls to mind a poem by Marianne Moore that Williams published in *Contact,* "Days of

Prismatic Color." In addition, a prism is a crystal. It also recalls an image from Williams's own essay on Moore: "Local color is not, as the parodists, the localists believe, an object of art. It is merely a variant serving to locate *acme point of white penetration*" (*SE* 122, emphasis mine). The lines from *Paterson* are in past tense—there *was* an earlier day of prismatic colors. Williams seems to be lamenting the loss of clarity—the "white penetration"—but he has substituted for the crystal his new luminosity, the "radiant gist."

At the same time, these lines raise the problem of origins, invoking as they do the image of his usually absent father.[15] In "Asphodel" (which was originally written as part of *Paterson,* book 5) he sees a man on the subway who looks like his father but is afraid to approach him: "Speak to him, / I cried. He / will know the secret" (*CP2* 329). He "did nothing about it"; after all, this was the same father who told him in a dream that his poetry was "no good" (*A* 14). Beyond the obvious Oedipal nature of these scenes there lurks another, deeply rooted issue. As has been observed by those who historicize Sigmund Freud, the problem of origin is particularly acute in nineteenth-century science—typified most obviously by Charles Darwin (who is mentioned in a key context in "Asphodel" and on the same page of the *Autobiography* referred to above).[16] The problem of origin intensified in the modern period (with the success of objective science) and is perhaps most evident in Williams's *In the American Grain,* a meditation on the beginning of the United States. But the issue of origin (and its relation to authority) is made problematic in Williams's later work—a point that is best elucidated by a brief look at Joseph Riddel's criticism of Williams and the work of T. S. Eliot, Williams's modernist nemesis.

In *The Inverted Bell* Riddel makes a case for Williams's postmodernism (though he tries to make much broader claims than I am attempting). At the heart of his argument are two ideas: texts that take themselves as their subject (and consequently lend themselves readily to analysis by Heideggerian or Derridian perspectives on "play") are already postmodern. More important is his assertion that postmodernism is a denial of origins—a point he attempts to demonstrate through a long reading of *Paterson.* This so-called problem of origin is another version of the problem of authority. We grant power to the first cause (Pasteur's anthrax bacillus, for example). If Williams can confront his father in his own old age, he can learn the secret (unveil the truth). The work of T. S. Eliot is also concerned with origins. *The Waste Land* is a searing indictment of the early modern period, and redemption is to be found in classical erudition and an understanding of the great sweep of Western myth—in other words, a return to the classical origins of Western high culture. But the authority of *The Waste Land* is not just the ancient texts; it invokes the erudite, urbane voice of the poet whose "individual talent" is to transmute these high cultural artifacts into new (but still timeless) art. Eliotic modernism has a double origin—one absent (the best that has been thought and said) and one present (the magisterial voice of the modern poet). Even though *The Waste Land* is fragmentary and, particularly on the first reading, impregnable, it holds out the possibility of reconstruction. Its references to other texts, end notes, and stolen quotations are possible keys for coherence, so the poem creates a *nostalgia* for origins. That is the distinction Riddel at times fails to emphasize in his discussion of *Paterson,* which is concerned with origin—history, local myth—but not with authority. Williams's voice (or the multiple voices he seems to quote at random) makes no pretense toward inclusive vision or magisterial pronouncement.[17]

The techniques of the two poems—*The Waste Land* and *Paterson*—underline this point. Both make extensive use of montage—Eliot quoting the masters and Williams quoting the man and woman on the street. Although it seems an inconsequential point, the difference is crucial for an understanding of Williams's late work and for some sense of the idea of postmodernism. Jameson makes a useful distinction: "At any rate, it becomes minimally obvious that the newer artists no longer 'quote' the materials, the fragments and motifs, of a mass or popular culture, as Flaubert began to do; they somehow incorporate them to the point where many of our older critical and evaluative categories (founded precisely on the radical differentiation of modernist and mass culture) no longer seem functional."[18] Eliot places multiple symbolic quotation marks around his cockney pub scene, while Williams quotes letters, scraps of conversation, and advertisements without implied comment. Henry Sayre makes a similar point when he argues that in book 5 of *Paterson* and in *Pictures from Brueghel* Williams is not concerned with "originality." Rather, he takes as his subject past art and presents his own interpretation. The difference between his and Eliot's work is a matter of tone. Williams offers *an* interpretation, Eliot gives *the* interpretation.[19] A primary characteristic ascribed to postmodern texts is an emphasis on the surface and a denial of depth; postmodernism is a horizontal rather than a vertical attitude. That is precisely the difference between the modern Eliot and the postmodern Williams. *The Waste Land* uses a rhetoric of depth, invites the reader to dig deep into the references to find the single glimmering truth contained in it. *Paterson* is a celebration of surface, a democracy of utterance, and a denial of the authority of high cultural origins: "the surface / glistens, only the surface. / Dig in—and you have / a nothing, surrounded by / a surface" (*P* 123).

Nevertheless, Williams's texts usually show a dialectic between the vertical and the horizontal, the modern and the postmodern. Mervyn LeRoy's 1944 film *Madame Curie* raises pointedly the metaphors of science—surface and depth—with which Williams struggled. Carol Donley has argued that Eve Curie's biography of her mother was an important source for *Paterson*.[20] I would add that Williams saw the MGM production in early 1944 and that the film, based on Eve Curie's text, contains all the specific references to Curie found in *Paterson*.[21] Perhaps more important, the film invites the conflation of scientific object and "beautiful thing," so it invokes the categories of the feminist critique of science discussed in chapter 4. The film documents Marie and Pierre Curie's discovery of radium, which on the surface is nearly the perfect practice of "masculine" science—the extraction of a single luminous object from tons of pitchblende. Throughout the film, however, the camera and lighting emphasize the face of Marie (played by Greer Garson), while Pierre (played by Walter Pidgeon) is usually shown in half light or a side view. While Marie focuses her eyes on the object of her science, the audience, which cannot see radium, looks at her. She becomes the radiant gist who always turns her face to the light—the literal trope of enlightenment.

Early on, Marie is an object to be conquered through science. Her soon-to-be-husband, Pierre, gives her an inscribed copy of his newly published scientific treatise just before his proposal. Throughout, he is depicted as stoic, methodical, and resolutely logical, while Marie shows emotional swings and, at the points where she is most insightful, is something of a poet. When they first see the photographic plate that proves pitchblende gives off rays, Pierre is analytical while; as the music comes up, Marie responds, "it is as if it were a piece of the sun locked up in here."[22] She is alternately depicted as a methodical scientist who produces a crucial discovery, a poet, a near saint, an emotional woman who must be supported by her husband in order to continue, and a luminous, beautiful thing oddly paralleling the object she pursues.

As if to underline Jordanova's contention that masculine science's primary activity is penetration, a dominant trope in the film is unveiling. The first major discovery (the postulation of radium as a new element) takes place when Marie opens a curtain covering a blackboard where she has written the chemical composition of pitchblende. Another occurs when they unveil the final evaporating dish after four years of crystallizing out the remaining elements. This move is profound, because they find nothing but a stain. The removal of the final veil reveals a void that only later, in the dark, can be seen as some*thing,* raising fundamental questions about the nature of a "thing" and making problematic notions of "objective" science.

Nineteenth-century materialist science was also being subverted by the developing understanding of the new physics. The relationship of radioactivity (the radiant gist) and Einstein's relativity plays a complicated role in Williams's post–World War II poems. Relativity was in the popular press by 1919, and Williams wrote "St. Francis Einstein of the Daffodils" in 1921. Still, it was not until late in that decade that he read Whitehead and Steinmetz[23] and came to a limited understanding of relativity. We must be sensitive to the historical specificity of relativity before we ascribe to it a wholesale influence on the modern period. Notions of speed and flow were important for the futurists and the vorticists, for example, or for Duchamp, but their celebration was of the technology of the age—the car and the cinema—and not an abstract mathematical theory. Even experimentation in narrative time can be attributed not to the new physics but rather to Henri Bergson and, perhaps more importantly, to new manufacturing and transportation technologies that not only defined the norm of time but also made it problematic. Broad popularization of Einstein's and the other major physicists' work did not occur until after the major artists of the modern period had long been at work. The revolution in physics can be said to parallel the other revolutions of the early part of the twentieth century, but direct influence, particularly on the early moderns, is tenuous at best.

In *Made in America,* Lisa Steinman is careful to distinguish the analogy of the machine from the new physics.[24] The first is a technical extension of Newtonian mechanics, while the latter is a wholesale reappropriation of mechanics on a highly abstract level.[25] To translate this difference into the terms of my discussion, the machine-age epistemological model is that of objectivist science, which depends on an observable, definable mechanical universe (what Whitehead called the nineteenth-century mechanical model). Williams was a man of this age. Even though he read Whitehead in 1927 and Steinmetz soon after and made some early references to Einstein and to poetry as "energy" (*Contact,* January 1921),[26] the relativity model did not make a strong impact on his work until after the explosion of the atomic bomb.[27]

If the culmination of the Newtonian model was the great machine age, the culmination of the new physics was Hiroshima. Even though, as Friedman and Donley carefully point out, Einstein's $E = mc^2$ was not the formula that enabled the construction of the bomb, the two were still tightly linked in the popular imagination. (They reproduce the cover of the 1 July 1946 *Time* magazine, which foregrounds the familiar shaggy head of Einstein with a mushroom cloud behind. On the cloud is written his famous formula.) The bomb was the physical representation of the new physics—it became a *local* detail. Most of the Williams texts that critics discuss in terms of relativity were written after Hiroshima— "The Poem as a Field of Action" (1948), the "variable foot" essays,[28] *Paterson,* "Asphodel"—and, to a great degree, coincide with the chronology of my argument. After the bomb, Williams began in earnest to abandon his "objective" epistemology, and the late poems document that struggle.

In the passages leading up to the first mention of the radiant gist (lines written almost ten years before the rest), Dr. Paterson is once again in hot pursuit of the "beautiful thing," his object of desire and the grail of his epic. He demands the woman disrobe, all the while insulting her for her filth: "You smell as though you need / a bath. Take off your clothes and purify / yourself" (*P* 105). The lines are punctuated with "(I said)," showing the clear authority of the speaking voice. He insists his gaze will purify her and perhaps himself:

> Give it up. Quit it. Stop writing.
> "Saintlike" you will never
> separate that stain of sense,
> (*P* 108)

This image of stains (similar to Marianne Moore's smudgeless words) leads him to Madam Curie: "—never separate that stain / of sense from the inert mass" (*P* 108). This radiance could still be that of the crystal, the object of scientific inquiry or the beautiful thing of aesthetic inquiry. As the writer of the epic *Paterson,* Williams must locate the luminous details in the inert mass of the texts he draws together. Like his alter ego Dev Evans, he must "shoot a clarity through the oppressing, obsessing murk of the world" (*VTP* 116). But radium loses electrons. It is an element that decays, and this instability creates dissonance—not just the "dissonance / in the valence of Uranium" (*P* 176), but also a dissonance in the objective epistemology.

Curie's gender and the importance of reproduction (which figures prominently in most of Williams's work) then becomes crucial:

> —a furnace, a cavity aching
> toward fission; a hollow,
> a woman waiting to be filled
>
> —a luminosity of elements, the
> current leaping!
> Pitchblende from Austria, the
> valence of Uranium inexplicably
> increased. Curie, the man, gave up
> his work to buttress her.
>
> But she is pregnant!
> (*P* 176)

Madam Curie is both the beautiful thing that gives off rays and the one person capable of understanding a phenomenon outside the epistemology of masculine science—an unstable object. In *The Visual Text of William Carlos Williams* Henry Sayre discusses in some detail Madam Curie and Williams's shifting attitude toward authority: "Her discovery is a metaphor for the discovery Williams himself had been seeking throughout the poem, and her method, he realizes, is his own: 'Love, the sledge that smashes the atom? No, No! antagonistic cooperation is the key' (*P* 177). This is an explicit denial of the dream of unity or, more precisely, of the dream that life is itself the realization of unity."[29] Love and radioactivity involve a denial of the Eliotic "still turning point" and instead demand a more dialectical, less authoritarian point of view. Williams's Curie is pregnant, ready to split like an atom (or atomic bomb), and her offspring casts doubts regarding the stability of the "real" world:

> Ah Madam!
> this is order, perfect and controlled
> on which empires, alas, are built
>
> But there may issue, a contaminant,
> some other metal radioactive
> a dissonance, unless the table lie,
> may cure the cancer . must
> lie in that ash . Helium plus, plus
> what?
>
> > (*P* 179)

He links uncertainty with Curie, but, more fundamentally, sets up a conflict between a knowable, objective world and one where the truths are uncertain, the objects are not exactly objects.[30] In other words, the nineteenth-century scientific epistemology in which Williams had been trained, and which had more or less stood him in good stead throughout his career, is slipping away. That loss perhaps accounts for the note of desperation in the "no ideas but in things" dictum. He is not simply attacking abstraction; he is clinging onto *things,* which are no longer quite stable.

This ambivalent attitude is expressed early in *Paterson* where Dr. Paterson finds himself in a static state, watching the others:

> Moveless
> he envies the men that ran
> and could run off
> toward the peripheries—
> to other centers, direct—
> for clarity (if
> they found it)
> > loveliness and
> authority in the world—
> > (*P* 36)

This sentiment becomes haunting at the beginning of *Paterson,*
book 5 (1958), where his familiar confidence quickly fades:

> In old age
>> the mind
>>>> casts off
>>> rebelliously
>> an eagle
> from its crag
>>>> —the angle of a forehead
>>> or far less
>> makes him remember when he thought
>>> he had forgot
>>>>> —remember
>>> confidently
>> only a moment, only for a fleeting moment—
>>>> with a smile of recognition . .
>>>>> (*P* 207)

Book 5 was written after Williams's stroke, which adds a poignancy to his flickering recognition, but what is significant here
is the tone of peaceful resignation. Throughout his work, Williams aggressively pursued an elusive "beautiful thing," seeking
to fix it clearly in his mind, but in the late poems he seems more
content with the flickering image, the little flecks of beauty that
are given off. Paul Bove has argued that in *Paterson* book 5, "the
poet not only refuses the movement back to an 'origin,' the sea
and its wrecks, but rejects as well the sirenic attractions of yielding consciousness and subjectivity, that is, authority, to an already
'present' death disguised as the great Mother. The poet must not
surrender entirely to matter."[31] In the late work Williams clearly
does not surrender to death, but that does not necessarily signal a
return to patriarchal authority. Terence Diggory, commenting on
Bove, argues "that Williams is continually yielding authority even
as he asserts it.[32] Diggory's point underlines Williams's struggle
in the late poems regarding both his age and an increasingly problematic epistemology.

In "The Orchestra" there is the uncertainty of the "wrong note,"
which is "not / a flute note either, it is the relation / of a flute note /
to a drum" (*CP2* 251),[33] and in "To Daphne and Virginia" uncertainty is expressed in sexual terms:

>   there is always
>   another, such as I,
>   who loves them,
>   loves all women, but
>   finds himself, touching them,
>   like other men,
>   often confused.
>   (*CP2* 247)

Rather than unveiling and penetrating, Williams touches these women while they are each penetrated by the odor of the boxwood. Even the doctor/poet is the passive recipient of the boxwood's "healing odor." Williams further undercuts his poetic as well as his masculine authority by comparing himself to a pet goose: "a very quiet old fellow / who writes no poems" (*CP2* 249).[34]

In "For Eleanor and Bill Monahan" (one of the first poems written after the 1952 stroke), he surrenders to the Virgin Mary. There is an element of parody as the opening lines invoke the Lord's Prayer and, at the same time, pagan fertility rituals. The mother of God becomes the many-women figure—from the mother/muse of "The Wanderer" to Kora to Phyllis and Corydon, Floss and his own mother, but the tone is remarkably submissive:

>   I do not come to you
>   save that I confess
>   to being
>   half man and half
>   woman. I have seen the ivy
>   cling
>   to a piece of crumbled
>   wall so that
>   you cannot tell
>   by which either
>   stands.
>   (*CP2* 253–54)

Williams admits his androgyny, something he does in the early work,[35] but more significantly, he stresses his inability to separate out specific objective facts. This Williams is not a beaten, tired poet, however. Rather, he is working through the conflict between enlightenment-based reason (masculine aggressiveness) and the "female principle of the world" (*CP2* 255).[36]

The poem that most typifies this conflict, "Asphodel, That Greeny

Flower," is suffused with images of both passivity and penetration. He opens apologetically but with an urgency, showing an acute sense of the loss of time but not dominated by a will to master or control it. The narrator (clearly Williams speaks in his own voice) instead "drinks" in his wife's approach—contains rather than penetrates her. The faint odor of the flower brings a flood of memories. It is not the silly odor of his earlier poem "Smell" (1917) where he berates his "strong-ridged and deeply hollowed / nose" for its insatiable curiosity (*CP1* 92). There his nose, like his eyes, is involved in the active penetration of nature's secrets. It is linked directly to knowledge: "Must you know everything?" The odor of "Smell" is desire, but the odor of the asphodel, similar to the boxwood in "To Daphne and Virginia," is "a moral odor" (*CP2* 312). It acts upon the narrator. He is penetrated and controlled by the lost world it invokes.

Among those memories are his more active, powerful roles:

> There had come to me
> a challenge,
> your dear self,
> mortal as I was,
> the lily's throat
> to the hummingbird!
> (*CP2* 313)

Here Williams the penetrator—the modernist Williams—pursues the secret or truth that the flower can reveal:

> I cannot say
> that I have gone to hell
> for your love
> but often
> found myself there
> in your pursuit.
> (*CP2* 314)

This pursuit is tied to voyages of aggression and exploration, which connects the image of the flower and the sea, and reminds him of "Helen's public fault" (*CP2* 315), the instigation of a bloody conflict—"those crimson petals / spilled among the stones"—and the beginning of all poetry. Thus flowers, the sea, and poetry are related to aggression, sex, and despoliation. Darwin's *Voyage of the Beagle* "opened our eyes / to the gardens of the world" (*CP2* 323), and Melville admired "some exotic orchid . . . in the / Hawaiian jungle" (329), which reminds the poet of another voyage:

> which promised so much
>   but due to the world's avarice
>   breeding hatred
> through fear,
>   ended so disastrously;
>   (*CP2* 323)[37]

He invokes many other images of authority and power—the statue of Colleoni's horse and Marsden Hartley's train—but, significantly, relates the flower to the atomic bomb, which brings destruction.

Williams's attitude toward the bomb is quite problematic.[38] He deplored the world it was creating, but at the same time it was the logical (if I may hazard that word in this context) extension of the modern period—the culmination of modern science. In "The Poem as a Field of Action" he says the "one great thing about 'the bomb' is the awakened sense it gives us that catastrophic (but why?) alterations are also possible in the human *mind,* in art" (*SE* 287). This statement touches the apocalyptic strain in Williams's work, which is related ideologically to the sanitation movement and military models of disease and immune response—both practices Williams understood and must have respected. The bomb could not simply remain for Williams a horror. It was also an object of fascination and potential (imaginary) purification.

"Asphodel," book 2, laments life in the atomic age—a world held hostage by this product of enlightenment science, which has become not an object of reason used judiciously but instead a pagan icon: "The mere picture / of the exploding bomb / fascinates us / so that we cannot wait / to prostrate ourselves / before it" (*CP2* 321–22). The flower of the Americas that increasingly sophisticated science and technology spoiled has become the destroyer, not just of an entire generation's peace of mind, but also of the promises enlightened science was supposed to fulfill.

At the end of book 3 he turns his metaphor of the flower around and around in order to encompass facts, imagination, poetry (simplicity, words), and love:

Don't think
that because I say this
in a poem
it can be treated lightly
or that the facts will not uphold it.
Are facts not flowers
and flowers facts
or poems flowers
or all works of the imagination,
interchangeable?
Which proves
that love
rules them all . . .
(*CP2* 333)

In *The Embodiment of Knowledge* Williams celebrates the imagination's ability to subsume all human activity beneath it. Here love, not the individual poet's mind, is the superior force.[39] This complex of images is carried over into the coda, where the gap between the flash and the thunderstroke creates the utopic moment of free play where a colt can "kick up his heels" and the bomb can be gelded. The life of the imagination, so frequently invoked throughout Williams's work, is no longer holding the object close to the nose (even though that is what he is doing with the flower); it is instead a surrendering to love and passivity:

So we come to watch time's flight
as we might watch
summer lightening
or fireflies, secure,
by grace of the imagination,
safe in its care.
(*CP2* 334–35)

He maintains confidence that "the light / for all time shall outspeed / the thunder crack" (*CP2* 335),[40] then ends with perhaps the most stunning lines of all his works:

At the altar
so intent was I
before my vows,
so moved by your presence
a girl so pale
and ready to faint

                    that I pitied
                              and wanted to protect you.
          As I think of it now,
                    after a lifetime,
                              it is as if
          a sweet-scented flower
                    were poised
                              and for me did open.
          Asphodel
                    has no odor
                              save to the imagination
          but it too
                    celebrates the light.
                              It is late
          but an odor
                    as from our wedding
                              has revived for me
          and begun again to penetrate
                    into all crevices
                              of my world.
                                        (*CP*2 336–37)

His memory of this event places him in a dominant role—one of
patriarch and protector—and Floss once again becomes a flower
opening for his penetration, but Williams's movement back to the
present creates different circumstances. The imagined odor of the
asphodel "celebrates the light," but it is not the aggressive light of
the speculum (or, on a more general level, enlightenment science), but instead the knotted trope of flowers, imagination, and
love, and the odor penetrates both Williams and "all the crevices
of [his] world."[41]

In a sense, Williams has simply adopted the classical image of
the poet inspired by the muse, but that reading ignores the complexity of the historical moment in which the poem was produced.
Williams, because of old age and ill health, had begun to doubt his
potency (both physical and verbal) and was consequently more
contemplative and less aggressive in his writing. But we must also
expand that sense of doubt to the broader social doubt experienced
by many in the Truman-Eisenhower era. The effects of an increasingly scientific medical education were being felt in the public's
developing sense of alienation from the medical profession. Hospitals and the AMA were discouraging the house calls that had
provided Williams with his all-important contact, and medical

professionals were becoming more aloof and separated from the lives of their patients. Even though scientific medicine was making enormous strides in diagnosis and therapeutics, a crisis was looming. Williams surely entertained doubts about the direction of his profession. He frequently decried doctors who were in it for the cash, and he supported socialized medicine (*Int* 51–52). The agony of Robert Oppenheimer was felt throughout the scientific community, and finally, the horrors of totalitarianism (both fascist and Stalinist) as they were revealed to Americans in the late 1940s and early 1950s cast considerable doubt on the modernist project, particularly since two of its major spokesmen—Williams's lifelong rival, T. S. Eliot, and lifelong friend, Ezra Pound—openly embraced versions of fascism as the only healthy atmosphere for the production of art.

Without doubt, "Asphodel" is the archetype of the confessional poem, and it is clearly related to Williams's personal circumstances. But there is something more fundamental about the tentativeness of his late work than the biological and directly personal. At key points in his texts Williams is participating in (and perhaps anticipating) today's critique of enlightenment science. The placebo effect is unsettling because it focuses scientists on a nonobjective phenomenon that produces material results- -a point that destabilizes objectivist hierarchies.

Another physician/writer, Axel Munthe, raises the question of medical semiology and simulation that returns our focus to the site of the utterance and the stage props necessary for its efficacy. *The Story of San Michel,* published in 1929, depicts Munthe as a physician reluctant to use his power to name (that which is not "objectively" there), but who finds it to his advantage. His women patients "seemed quite upset when I told them that they looked rather well and their complexion was good, but they rallied rapidly when I added that their tongue looked rather bad—as seemed generally to be the case. My diagnosis, in most cases was over-eating, too many cakes or sweets during the day or too heavy dinners at night. It was probably the most correct diagnosis I ever made in those days, but it met with no success. Nobody wanted to hear anything more about it, nobody liked it. What they all liked was appendicitis."[42] When appendicitis faded as the fashionable Parisian disease, "a new complaint had to be discovered to meet the general demand. The Faculty was up to the mark, a new disease was dumped on the market, a new word was coined, a gold coin indeed, COLITIS! It was a neat complaint, safe from the surgeon's knife, always at hand when wanted, suitable to everybody's taste. Nobody knew when it came, nobody knew when it went away."[43] He describes his acquisition of a new patient and subsequent entrée into Parisian society: "The Marquise wished to know at once all the symptoms of colitis and smiled cheerfully at me while I dripped the subtle poison down the ear-trumpet. When I stood up to go, I had lost my voice, but I had found a new patient."[44] We must assume he lost his voice out of professional embarrassment, but what his aphasia signals is the very power of that voice. The naming of a disease is not so much an enlightenment as it is a social phenomenon usually keyed toward some exercise of power or control.

In "The Use of Force" the doctor reads a series of texts—the parent's fear, the child's reticence, recent cases of diphtheria in the area—but then confirms diagnosis with a master code or sign: the throat culture. For this doctor, it is still possible to prove the objective reality of a diagnosis—to show that the naming of the disease was appropriate. In *Paterson* Corydon names the rocks in the harbor her "sheep" (*P* 152), but, as Phyllis tells us, they are just rocks white with gull crap. The modernist physicians' version of reality is "real"—not simulation—because they (Munthe and Williams' narrator) have behind them the mechanisms of modern science: the ideology of clarity and the theater of proof, as well as a two-thousand-year tradition of knowledge and expertise. Postmodern Corydon, a socially marginalized figure, has money but little else to force more than limited assent to her version of the truth, to her act of naming.

In "Danse Russe" (1916) young Doc Williams celebrates his loneliness by dancing naked by himself before the mirror. He challenges anyone to contest his naming of himself:

> Who shall say I am not
> the happy genius of my household?
> (*CP1* 87)

One of his last poems, "The Dance" (published in 1962), asks a significantly different question: "there are always two, / yourself and the other" (*CP2* 407):

> But only the dance is sure!
> make it your own.
> Who can tell
> what is to come of it?
> (*CP2* 408)[45]

This latter Williams is not alone. He is not a representative of the "sovereign profession," nor a magisterial modern master. He is *part* of a community (a community of two) and can only voice with any certainty his own uncertainty.

Notes

Introduction

1. Early in his practice, Williams made his rounds in a horse and buggy (Mariani, *New World,* 98). Electric light was developed in 1892, load-bearing concrete walls in 1892, sealed ventilation between 1903 and 1906, and the first Model T rolled off the assembly line in 1908.

2. In recent years Cecelia Tichi and Lisa Steinman have examined the general adoption of scientific and technological tropes in modern literature, and this study is very much in their debt. From a Marxist perspective, Stanley Aronowitz has argued that scientific power is not just coercion or institutional domination; rather, it exceeds specific institutional sites because of the pervasiveness of science in *all* discourses.

3. Starr, *Social Transformation,* 110.

4. Or, as John Harley Warner has argued, "medicine did not simply become more scientific during the nineteenth century; what was considered science, and what was not, changed" (*Therapeutic Perspective,* 7).

5. In *The Care of Strangers,* Charles Rosenberg notes that the Flexner report was the culmination of an ongoing reform movement (209); consequently, many of the issues raised were already anticipated and addressed by the major medical schools.

6. Williams, *Autobiography,* 286. All further references to Williams's work will be made parenthetically in the text. See p. ix for a list of title abbreviations.

7. See, for example, *The Early Poetry of William Carlos Williams,* where Rod Townley examines Williams's "split-psyche."

8. In "Give Me a Laboratory and I Will Raise the World," Bruno Latour examines the rhetorical power of the inside/outside distinction in scientific discourse, arguing that that distinction, while quite powerful, has no scientific basis.

9. This is not to imply that medicine ever occupied a utopic, altruistic space sometime in the distant past, only that the nostalgic attitude projects just such a past as a critique of the "degraded" present.

10. "Certainly his prevailing sense of 'outsiderliness' was reenforced by his

loneliness at home [1927]. He also realized that he could not really adopt for himself or his art anything like an avant-garde flourishing of alienation. He needed Flossie, his medical work, his income, his feet on familiar ground: at the same time he pushed forward to express his inability to accept any or all of these rootings as sufficient occasion for his writing" (Duffey, *Poetry of Presence,* 141).

11. Fleck, *Genesis,* 39. Fleck's concepts bear a strong resemblance to Kuhn's paradigms *(The Structure of Scientific Revolutions)* and Foucault's discursive formations *(The Archaeology of Knowledge).*

12. Ibid., 99.

13. See Jean-François Lyotard, *The Postmodern Condition,* chapter 3.

14. See, for example, the feminist critique of science, the Frankfurt school's work, as well as Kuhn, Feyerabend, Latour, and the social studies of science and technology. See in particular Joseph Rouse, *Knowledge and Power,* chapter 7.

15. Latour, *Pasteurization,* 221.

16. In *Science in Action* Latour argues that "Nature is the final cause of the settlement of all controversies, *once controversies are settled.* As long as they last *Nature will appear simply as the final consequence of the controversies"* (98).

17. This part of his thought is derived in part from his alignment with the work of Michel Serres and is explained in some detail in "Postmodern? No, Simply Amodern: Steps Towards an Anthropology of Science" and "One More Turn after the Social Turn: Easing Science Studies into the Non-Modern World."

18. By this I do not mean that science is false. Rather, by doubting the methods of science as a special way of knowing the world, we can begin to understand just how much its cultural authority rests on the discourse it uses and the image it projects. By working at it backward—through literature rather than scientific texts—it is possible to see where numerous networks overlap and, through that association, exert power. (For a discussion of the literary strategies of scientific texts, see Karin Knorr-Cetina, *The Manufacture of Knowledge,* and the work of the Edinburgh school.)

1. Authority, Honesty, and Charisma

1. Paul Starr's term; see *The Social Transformation of American Medicine.*

2. Clendening, *Source Book,* 20.

3. Ibid., 46.

4. Ibid., 47.

5. Starr, *Social Transformation,* 34; see also John Harley Warner, *The Therapeutic Perspective,* and Charles Rosenberg, *The Care of Strangers.*

6. Ibid., 110.

7. On the authority of science in Williams's texts, see Steinman, *Made in America,* 2, passim.

8. In many of his short stories, Williams's narrator is a rural/suburban practitioner going about his profession within an immigrant community—in short, a doctor much like Williams himself.

9. William Osler's *Principles and Practice of Medicine* (1918) defines mucous

colitis as "a secretion neurosis of the large intestine met with particularly in nervous and hysterical patients. It is more common in women than in men. It has increased greatly of late years, and has become the fashionable complaint, displacing neuritis to a great extent" (551).

10. A chauvinism that indeed is part of the medical examination. Medical practice is gendered through the construction of this scene of knowledge production, a point to be examined in chapter 4.

11. Quoted in Osler, *Evolution of Modern Medicine*, 78.

12. "Discourse on Language," 221-24.

13. There is some doubt as to the author of the text *Arnaldi de Villa Nova de cautelis medicorum*. Some speculate that Arnauld simply copied parts from another text ([Arnauld], *De cautelis medicorum*, 131-34).

14. Ibid., 135.

15. Osler, *Selected Writings*, 184.

16. Mona Van Duyn in "To 'Make Light of It' as Fictional Technique" argues that the last line is ironic: "He points out that a choice of the Communist diagnosis and treatment for society's ills would be, after all, no more mistaken than their own attempt to diagnose and treat the child's had been" (238). Williams often expressed an interest and a sympathy for the Russian revolution. It seems the line is not a denigration of the Soviet experience but instead compares the futility of the poor's situation in Hell's Kitchen to the likelihood of a strong American Communist party.

17. Quoted in Flexner, *Medical Education in the United States*, 4.

18. Rush, *Selected Writings*, 305.

19. Flexner, *Medical Education in the United States*, 26.

20. Cited in Terrell, *Man and Poet*, 391.

21. Poirier, "The Physician and Authority," 28.

22. Williams was not above using the authority granted him by both his professions. In a letter to *The Freeman* (23 June 1920) he expresses outrage against the legal system's handling of the case of John Coffey. Williams establishes himself as both a writer and a physician and, having developed this twofold authority, is in a position to offer an informed opinion regarding Coffey's sanity. In *Kora in Hell* Williams inverts Galen's lesson. Maxwell Bodenheim showed up in New York with what appeared to be an injured shoulder and duped his fellow writers into a month's free room and board. According to Williams, "the joint was done up in a proper Sayre's dressing and there really looked to be a bona-fide injury" (27). He marvels at Bodenheim's ability as a writer and his straight-forward egotism, but perhaps most at his ability to get one over on a trained physician. Bogie-fooling some ignorant poets is one thing, but a worldly doctor is quite another.

23. See George Monteiro's "Doc Rivers, Rogue Physician" on Rivers as scapegoat embodying both the best and the worst traits of his society (56).

24. See also Guenter Risse, "From Horse and Buggy to Automobile and Telephone."

25. For a view of the ethical implications of Rivers's behavior, see Willms and Schneiderman, "The Ethics of Impaired Physicians."

26. In 1890 Osler called Freiburg the "most progressive" postgraduate medical institution in the world (*Selected Writings*, 161).

27. In the first code of ethics adopted by the AMA in 1847, much attention is given to the proper behavior of physicians in relation to one another regarding consultation. The code is clear in its concern about physicians impugning in public the abilities of other practitioners; consequently, most cases of malpractice were to be administered internally by the members of the profession (with minimal publicity).

28. Bernard, *Experimental Medicine*, 42.

29. He goes on to describe science in terms remarkably close to Eliot's conception of the poet in "Tradition and the Individual Talent": "Physics and chemistry, as established sciences, offer us the independence and impersonality which the experimental method demands" (Bernard, *Experimental Medicine*, 43).

30. Ibid, 43.

31. A point well illustrated by the life and work of T. S. Eliot.

2. *Against Theory: The Rhetoric of Clarity*

1. Pound, *Literary Essays*, 3.
2. Ibid., 11.
3. Zukofsky, *Prepositions*, 21.
4. Ibid., 25.
5. Flexner, *Medical Education in the United States*, 210.
6. Abbott, *Principles of Bacteriology*, 18.
7. Pellegrino, *Medicine and Literature*, xv.
8. Boroff, "Diagnostic Eye," 65.
9. Fleck, *Genesis*, 35–36.
10. Ibid., 42.
11. Osler, *The Evolution of Modern Medicine*, 68.
12. Ibid., 98, passim.
13. Heseler, *Vesalius' First Public Anatomy*, 273.
14. Clendening, *Source Book*, 219.
15. Ibid., 307.
16. Ibid., 315.
17. Pinel, *Clinical Training*, 69.
18. Ibid., 73.
19. Warner, *Therapeutic Perspective*, 46. See chapter 2 for a detailed discussion of the antitheoretical movement in nineteenth-century American medicine.
20. Virchow, *Cellular Pathology*, 72.
21. Warner, *Therapeutic Perspective*, 244.
22. Bernard, *Experimental Medicine*, 35.
23. Ibid., 37.
24. Welch, *Addresses*, 13.
25. Ibid., 16.
26. Ibid., 17.
27. Today scientific medical education has come under fire, and schools have responded by including the humanities as required courses or, as Harvard is doing with New Pathways, getting the students in contact with patients during the first two years rather than using that time exclusively for laboratory studies.

28. Flexner, *Medical Education in the United States,* 156.

29. See, for example, the exchange of letters between Williams and Louis Grundin regarding Williams's essay on Gertrude Stein (Mariani, *New World,* 301–2).

30. Kuhn, *Structure of Scientific Revolutions,* 10–11.

31. Latour develops a more sophisticated version of paradigms with Actor-Network theory. In essence, he shows how scientific practice proceeds along possible paths and through various nodes by a trajectory made possible because of action by both the actors and the networks.

32. Or, from an opposite perspective, the frameworks can be said to construct the object. Fleck notes that, according to Citron, "cognition should progress not through intuition or from empathy with the phenomena as a whole, but through clinical and laboratory observation of the various constituent phenomena. The so-called diagnosis—the fitting of a result into a system of distinct disease entities—is the goal, and this assumes that such entities actually exist, and that they are accessible to the analytical method" (*Genesis,* 63–64).

33. Warner, *Therapeutic Perspective,* 58.

34. Reiser, *Medicine in the Reign of Technology,* 19.

35. Williams's sense of the machine is examined in more detail in chapters 5 and 6.

36. Pound, *Literary Essays,* 3.

3. A Theater of Proof

1. Shapin, *Isis,* 375.

2. Fleck, *Genesis,* 117. See also Aronowitz, *Science as Power* 328.

3. Pinel, *Clinical Training,* 68.

4. Orwell, *Orwell Reader,* 88.

5. Nightingale, *Notes on Hospitals,* 12.

6. Welch, *Addresses,* 127.

7. Stanley Joel Reiser notes that the University of Pennsylvania and Harvard were two of the few schools to have microscope labs by the 1870s (*Medicine in the Reign of Technology,* 81).

8. Foucault, *The Birth of the Clinic,* 107.

9. Shapin, *Isis,* 373–74.

10. Bernard, *Experimental Medicine,* 103.

11. For a broad philosophic treatment of this issue, see Foucault, "The Discourse on Language." On the particulars of current laboratory practice, see Latour and Woolgar, *Laboratory Life,* and Knorr-Cetina, *The Manufacture of Knowledge.*

12. Fleck discusses in some detail the difficulties encountered in trying to reproduce the Wassermann reaction with any consistency, and most medical laboratory breakthroughs have been difficult to reproduce at other sites with other audiences (a phenomenon that lends some weight to the mid-nineteenth-century conception of *specificity*). Latour's *Pasteurization of France* explores the difficulty the Pasteurian method had crossing international borders.

13. In *Knowledge and Power* Joseph Rouse argues that science seems univer-

sal because its tools become standardized and therefore reproducible (113). In the middle of the twentieth century, the U.S. Public Health Service was particularly proud of its portable laboratories (Mullan, *Plagues and Politics,* 36, 58).

14. For a longer discussion of this perspective, see T. Hugh Crawford, "Give Me Fragile Networks and I Will Raise the World," *Critical Texts* 7.1 (1990): 29–39.

15. Latour, *Pasteurization,* 85.

16. Advocates of clinical medicine would argue that the rendering of the object visible is in itself a relatively passive act, hardly the power structure Latour describes. They would call on nature to substantiate the claim that science merely describes an orderly phenomenal world. Latour does not deny that microbes exist; however, he does not allow them to exist as "objects" outside of the very specific context in which they are isolated and manipulated.

17. Latour, *Pasteurization,* 86.

18. In his introduction to the journal, Steven Ross Loevy argues that Williams's understanding of the "aesthetic dimension of medicine" originated in sections of "Rome." Medicine as an aesthetic perspective (either conscious or unconscious) pervades Williams's writing long before 1924, however.

19. Foucault, *The Birth of the Clinic,* 114.

20. Ibid., 115.

21. In discussing the data derived from new medical technologies, Stanley Joel Reiser notes that "one of the problems lay in the fact that the physician still found it hard to transpose into words the information received by touch, and then to adequately communicate the message to others" (*Medicine in the Reign of Technology,* 103). Koch pioneered the use of photography to disseminate views of bacteria because description and duplication were so difficult (ibid., 89–90).

22. Johns, *Eakins,* 55.

23. Ibid., 79.

24. Much of Eakins's work shows his fascination with things mechanical. Many of his early drawings detail machine parts or tools, as do several of his more famous paintings (including the two clinic paintings and his sketches for *William Rush Carves His Allegorical Statue*).

25. The role of the nurse as the only woman (except the patient) present in a scene of knowledge production for men is significant. Unlike *The Gross Clinic,* where the woman (presumably the young man's mother) is clearly distressed, this nurse is in calm control of the situation, and her assuredness typifies the model of the "strong" woman Williams explored often in his fiction and auto-biographies. With her steady eye trained on the incision, she becomes a counter to the authority of Dr. Agnew and the scene. The arrangement calls into question the patriarchal nature of scientific knowledge, an issue to be discussed in the next chapter.

26. Fried, *Realism,* 65.

27. Many critics have discussed Williams's relationship to Sheeler and preci-sionism; see Bram Dijstra, Paul Mariani, Rick Stewart, and Henry Sayre, to name a few.

28. Sontag, *On Photography,* 7.

29. Lucic, *Sheeler,* 118.

30. On Williams and photography, see Schmidt, *William Carlos Williams, the Arts, and Literary Tradition,* 20–21.

31. Lucic, *Sheeler,* 111.

32. Foucault, *Birth of the Clinic,* 95.

33. "Between Walls" can be seen as an "urban pastoral." For an extended discussion of this idea and its relation to precisionism, see Schmidt, *William Carlos Williams, the Arts, and Literary Tradition,* chapter 1.

34. In *Paterson,* book 3, Williams combines the image of the bottle with the furnace:

> A bottle, mauled
> by the flames, belly bent with laughter
>
> . . . .
> The beauty of fire-blasted sand
> that was glass, that was a bottle: unbottled.
> Unabashed. So be it.
>
> (117)

He welcomes the violence of the fire and the sights it provides. His pun on "abashed" undercuts the potential violence of a broken bottle, but at the same time provides the object with its own assertiveness.

35. This aspect of the painting calls to mind Marcel Duchamp's infamous "found" sculpture *Fountain,* which scandalizes on more levels than the obvious. His crudely painted signature, "R. Mutt," resembles graffiti, and of course, a public urinal is often the site where graffiti appears.

4. Feminism, Clarity, and Unveiling

1. "The Great Sex Spiral," *The Egoist* (April 1917), 46.

2. "The Great Sex Spiral," *The Egoist* (August 1917), 111.

3. Weaver, *American Background,* 25. On this relationship see also Mazarro, *Later Poems,* 120, passim.

4. Audrey Rogers's *Virgin and Whore,* Kerry Driscoll's *William Carlos Williams and the Maternal Muse,* and Marjorie Perloff's "The Man Who Loved Women," to name just a few.

5. Sandra Harding, *The Science Question in Feminism,* 9.

6. See also Harding, *The Science Question;* Donna Haraway, *Primate Visions;* Jacobus, Keller, and Shuttleworth, eds., *Body/Politics;* and Ruth Bleier, ed., *Feminist Approaches to Science.*

7. Keller, *Reflections on Gender and Science,* 36–37.

8. For example, in medicine this model often excludes from consideration environmental issues or psychological states when determining in the laboratory the cause of a specific disease. It also makes scientists, in their search for the "magic bullet," reluctant to look to alternative approaches such as the viral/bacterial synergistic model proposed as the cause of AIDS.

9. Jordanova, *Sexual Visions,* 87.

10. Showalter, *Sexual Anarchy,* 145.

11. Quoted in Jordanova, *Sexual Visions,* 28.

12. Ibid., 28–29.

13. In "The Woman as Operator" (1948) he says, "There's really nothing much to man aside from what he does, what he knows, what he desires or makes. Take those away and you have no man. But woman, that's something else again. It appears even at the height of voluptuous enjoyment as something unassailable. There's nothing to be done with it. To a man the more loving and willing she is and the more she gives herself, the more remote she becomes to him" (*RI* 180).

14. In a different context, Howard Berliner defines medicine in telling terms: "By the term medicine, I refer to the theory and practice of healing in which: (1) invasive manipulations are used to restore/maintain the human organism at a statistically determined equilibrium; (2) the patient's role is largely passive and the healing is accomplished through external means; (3) ill health and disequilibrium are assumed to be materially generated by specific elements such as bacteria, viruses, genetic malformations, parasites, etc. and can be empirically observed" ("Medical Modes of Production," 162).

15. Jordanova, *Sexual Visions,* 91.

16. Clendening, *Source Book,* 103.

17. Reiser, *Medicine in the Reign of Technology,* 55.

18. Leavitt, *Brought to Bed,* 41.

19. Reiser, *Medicine in the Reign of Technology,* 55. This tendency was begun with Giovanni Battista Morgagni's *On the Seats and Causes of Diseases* (1761), which moved away from notions of humoral balance to the search for the specific site of disease.

20. See William Marling's "Corridor to a Clarity" for an extended discussion of this passage.

21. In particle physics this is exemplified by Heisenberg's famous uncertainty principle.

22. Mariani, *New World,* 253.

23. Weaver, *American Background,* 23.

24. Lentricchia, "Patriarchy," 766.

25. Jerome Mazarro discusses the relation of Williams's poetry to masculinity in similar terms (*Later Poems,* chapter 4), as does Steinman (*Made in America,* 14–34, 136); see also Gilbert, "Purloined Letters".

26. At the end of *In the American Grain,* Lincoln is described in unique terms:

> It is Lincoln pardoning the fellow who slept on sentry duty. It is the grace of the Bixby letter. The least private would find a woman to caress him, a woman in an old shawl—with a great bearded face and a towering black hat above it, to give unearthly reality.
>
> Brancusi should make his statue—of wood—after the manner of his Socrates, with a big hole in the enormous mass of the head, save that this would be a woman. (234)

Williams creates an androgynous hero to finish his book, which is history (read masculine) yet impressionistic (read feminine). For a discussion of sexuality in *In the American Grain,* see Bryce Conrad's "Engendering History."

27. In the "Rome" journal (perhaps the most obscenely antagonistic of his writings), he turns his indignation on the Romans, but more generally on the

tradition represented by the eternal city: "The Romans saw—Men bugger each other, sometimes their assholes bleed or burn, their pricks come out with shit on them. What of it—they liked it but most of them are sons of bitches—white-livered incapable bastards that do not dare suck off a sleeping child—they are so frightened" (44). The irony of this passage is heightened when compared to Marcia Nardi's letters in *Paterson* where she accuses him of having lived an overly "safe" life (see in particular book 2).

28. See Driscoll, *Maternal Muse,* 5.

29. Foucault, *History of Sexuality* 1:59–60.

30. Perloff, "The Man Who Loved Women," 841.

31. In " 'The Use of Force' and First Principles of Medical Ethics" Barbara Currier Bell surveys the criticism, seeing two main lines of interpretation: (1) the doctor is bad; this is an example of unethical behavior (including the rape interpretation); (2) the doctor is human, just doing a difficult job under difficult circumstances. She finally sees it as a story that questions the motives of those who choose to study medicine, relating that choice to will and to power (*Literature and Medicine* 3, 143–51).

32. She also assaults his patriarchal authority on a more fundamental level. As Terence Diggory notes, her scratching at his eyes is a symbolic castration (*Ethics of Painting,* 57).

33. Williams's admiration for young girls is often sexual. In "The Girl with the Pimply Face" the narrator says, "Boy, she was tough and no kidding but I fell for her immediately" (*FD* 117). He goes on, "But after all she wasn't such a child. She had breasts you knew would be like small stones to the hand, good muscular arms and fine hard legs" (*FD* 119). See also "William Carlos Williams and the Singular Woman," where Joan Nay discusses some of the more troubling poems about young girls, e.g., "The Ogre," "Sympathetic Portrait of a Child."

34. Jean-François Lyotard discusses this phenomenon: "I would like to call a differend [*différend*] the case where the plaintiff is divested of the means to argue and becmes for that reason a victim. If the addressor, the addressee, and the sense of the testimony are neutralized, everything takes place as if there were no damages. . . . A case of differend between two parties takes place when the 'regulation' of the conflict that opposes them is done in the idiom of one of the parties while the wrong suffered by the other is not signified in that idiom" (*The Differend,* 9).

35. Gilbert, "Purloined Letters," 7.

36. This point is examined in more detail in chapter 6.

37. Fleck, *Genesis,* 42.

38. See Kerry Driscoll's *William Carlos Williams and the Maternal Muse* on the importance of Williams's mother in his work and life.

5. Someone to Drive the Car: Technology, Medicine, and Modernism

1. Cecelia Tichi has discussed the use of some of these terms (e.g., *speed* and *efficiency*) in the writing of many moderns and also has shown their value-

laden quality in the popular press as well as magazine advertisements: "Maintain Your Efficiency by Smoking Tuxedo—The Mildest, Pleasantest Tobacco Made" (*Shifting Gears,* 85). She notes a paragraph in the introduction to Strunk and White's *The Elements of Style* (attributed to Strunk in 1919): "Vigorous writing is concise. A sentence should contain no unnecessary words, a paragraph no unnecessary sentences, for the same reason that a drawing should have no unnecessary lines and a machine no unnecessary parts" (224). On the relation of the arts to the machine in this era, see Richard Guy Wilson et al., *The Machine Age in America,* and Jeffrey Meikle, *Twentieth Century Limited.*

2. On the rise of the hospital, see Charles E. Rosenberg, *The Care of Strangers,* and Morris J. Vogel, *The Invention of the Modern Hospital.*

3. On the influence of the car and the telephone on medicine, see Paul Starr, *The Social Transformation of American Medicine;* Stanley J. Reiser, *Medicine and the Reign of Technology;* and Guenter Risse, "From Horse and Buggy to Automobile and Telephone."

4. In 1914 the *Journal of the Medical Society of New Jersey* stated: "The Official State Medical Journals are not ashamed of their advertisements; hence they urge their readers to patronize their advertisers. The publishers believe it is their duty to the readers as well as the advertisers to bring them together. *The California State Journal of Medicine* has very truly said: 'There was a time, not so many years age, when no respectable publication would refer to its advertisements, or its advertisers. Now, however, all that has been changed; *we are proud of our advertisers* and our advertising' " (698).

5. *Charlotte Medical Journal* 2.2 (April 1915): 344.

6. *Journal of Nervous and Mental Disease* 38 (1911): vii.

7. Even tire ads were directed toward physicians. In 1914 Sterling advertised a snap-on tread—a do-it-yourself recap—that was inexpensive, convenient, and quick (*Journal of the Medical Society of New Jersey* 11.11 (November 1914): 1). On the relation of time to labor and machinery, see E. P. Thompson's seminal essay "Time, Work-Discipline, and Industrial Capitalism." On these issues in relation to modern art, see Stephen Kern's *Culture of Time and Space.*

8. See Sayre, "American Vernacular," 314; also Tichi and Steinman.

9. Latour, *Science in Action,* 174–75.

10. Pacey, *Culture of Technology,* chapter 3.

11. Heidegger, *Question,* 13.

12. Alan Trachtenberg notes: "Technological determinism implied that machines demanded their own improvement, that they controlled the forms of production and drove their owners and workers. Americans were taught to view their machines as independent agencies of power, causes of 'progress' " (*Incorporation of America,* 54–55).

13. The double nature of this paradigm was pointed out to me by Richard Grusin.

14. In a sense, they treat the world as what Heidegger calls "standing reserve." The instrumentalist view is that technology treats its raw materials (including humans) as simple resources to be used. Technology (and perhaps Williams's poetry) transforms nature and all it contains into "standing reserve"—the ultimate instrumentalist view.

15. If technology is a social organization of forces, then the need for the doctor to use a car in his practice is part of medical technology.

16. Roy Miki discusses the correlation between the automobile and Williams's improvisational style in *The Prepoetics of William Carlos Williams,* chapter 8.

17. A point discussed in chapter 7.

18. Many of his letters show his desire to make poetry at least equivalent to work esteemed by the American public. For example, in one to Louis Zukofsky he refers to himself as a "laborer," and to Kenneth Burke he says, "Yes, medicine pays. Bless your heart, it is easy for me to admire you, surrounded as I am with paying dirt in the form of grippe, tonsillitis. Each to his own filth" (*SL* 54).

19. Usually "Fine Work" is read as a celebration of an Old World sense of craftsmanship set up against the "shoddy" of American manufacture. It is important to note, however, that the laborers in this poem are working on the coping of a flat roof—the signature of many modern architects (particularly Le Corbusier). On this poem, see Sayre, "American Vernacular."

20. Riddel, *The Shaken Realist,* 63.

21. Here again Latour is a useful gloss on Williams's text. In *The Pasteurization of France* he argues that we should not privilege human actors in order to explain change or innovation (35). Instead, he prefers the idea of agents (human or nonhuman) that form alliances along networks. Although here Williams is being flippant, his construction of a nonhuman main character is significant.

22. In *A Novelette* (a text quite similar to *The Great American Novel*) Williams calls attention to the first great interchangeable-part technology—the alphabet—which he then displays in the order of a modern invention, the typewriter: "qwerty . . ." (*I* 282).

23. In a sense, *The Great American Novel* simply calls attention to its own bricolage. Lévi-Strauss's distinction does not hold up under scrutiny, as many sociological studies of technoscience have shown. For example, Latour's early study of the laboratory *(Laboratory Life)* shows that often experiments are designed (cobbled together) because the laboratory just happened to have a particular instrument or access to a specific sample.

24. Anne Janowitz makes a similar point in "*Paterson:* An American Contraption," where she depicts T. S. Eliot's model for the poet as a "white-coated laboratory researcher mixing emotions to find new objective correlatives," while Williams's could be found "puttering around the garage: adding and adjusting bits of machinery to make a new poem-invention" (301).

25. Tichi discusses human-machine medical metaphors (*Shifting Gears,* 34–40, 273–79).

26. James Tyson, with whom Williams studied at the University of Pennsylvania Medical School, discusses neurasthenia in his *Practice of Medicine* (a text Williams used): "It is distinctive of neurasthenia as contrasted with hysteria that it is more frequent among men, on whom business care and financial worry fall more severely. It is well known that men differ greatly in their power to bear the mental strain incident to the struggle for existence or business success. From the special prevalence of this disease in America, it has been called the 'American Disease,' and is reasonably ascribable to the fact that mental and physical strength in this country is more taxed than in any other" (1079).

27. Lisa Steinman and Henry Sayre both call attention to the relationship between Williams's poem as machine and Le Corbusier's houses, which are machines for living. Le Corbusier's *Toward a New Architecture* (discussed in chapter 8) envisions architecture as an alternative to revolution because well-designed housing (modeled on the clean, efficient lines of the machine) could solve the problems of the modern city.

28. See Williams's "Basis of Faith in Art" for an extended discussion of architecture and social planning between Williams and his brother, Edgar (who was an architect).

29. On this concept, see Howard P. Segal's *Technological Utopianism in American Culture*. In 1933 Harold Loeb, an acquaintance of Williams, published a technological utopia entitled *Life in a Technocracy: What It Might Be Like*.

30. Mumford repeats this diagnosis in his essay "The City," in Harold Stearn's *Civilization in the United States*.

31. Heidegger, *Question*, 25.

6. An Ideology of Cleanliness

1. One cannot simply look at poor sanitation alone as cause for high mortality. Other contributing factors were the condition of those admitted (most hospitals were patronized by the indigent) and the lack of therapeutically efficacious treatment. See Rosenberg, *Care of Strangers;* Vogel, *Invention of the Modern Hospital;* and Warner, *Therapeutic Perspective.*

2. Francis, *Hospital Hygiene,* 160, 191.

3. Florence Nightingale never accepted germ theory, at least in part because it, like the "masculine" science discussed in chapter 4, isolated the single cause of a disease rather than addressing the broad circumstances of life and health.

4. A good discussion of the relationship between the medical establishment and childbirth is Judith Walzer Leavitt's *Brought to Bed: Childbearing in America, 1750–1950.* She argues that doctors were invited into the birthing room throughout much of the nineteenth century, but really did not begin to control the process until birth became a "hospital-centered medical event" (5). See also Treichler, "Feminism, Medicine, and the Meaning of Childbirth."

5. Hirst, *Text-Book of Obstetrics,* 170. To be fair to Hirst, he defines labor as "the process by which a female expels from her uterus and vagina the ovum at its period of full maturity" (171). Paula Treichler quotes a contemporary obstetrics textbook where the "female" doesn't even make an appearance: "[Normal] labor is the physiologic process by which the uterus expels or attempts to expel its contents" ("Feminism, Medicine, and the Meaning of Childbirth," 122).

6. Hirst, *Text-Book of Obstetrics,* 170.

7. The parallels between these illustrations and Picabia's mechanomorphs were probably not lost on Williams.

8. Leavitt, *Brought to Bed,* 43.

9. Leavitt demonstrates that the mortality rates between hospital and home births in the 1930s were not significantly different. The hospital might have better equipment, but at this point in history (before the advent of antibiotics) it cannot provide significantly better care.

10. The pastoralizing of technology is a particularly vital rhetoric in American texts from the late ninteenth century to the present. From Emily Dickinson's "I like to see it lap the miles" to contemporary four-wheel-drive truck commercials, writers, advertisers, and filmmakers exploit a nostalgia for a pretechnological age, all the while presenting to the audience state-of-the-art machinery.

11. Tichi quotes Flexner on the role of the hospital in medical education, emphasizing (somewhat poetically) "the 'efficient and intelligent routine' of the 'hospital machine' " (*Shifting Gears*, 273).

12. *Charlotte Medical Journal* 2.2 (April 1915): xxii.

13. Quoted in Steinman, *Made in America*, 79.

14. Tichi, *Shifting Gears*, 260.

15. On the modernization of the kitchen, see Siegfried Geidion, *Mechanization*, 512–27.

16. Jerome Mazarro relates the importance of language in science (since experiments must be communicated clearly) to Williams's writing (*Later Poems*, 10).

17. Cushman, *Meanings of Measure*, 22.

18. Flexner, *Medical Education: A Comparative Study*, 3.

19. He praises Poe in similar terms: "The language of his essays is a remarkable HISTORY of the locality he springs from. There is no aroma to his words, rather a luminosity, that comes of a disassociation from anything else than thought and ideals" (*IAG* 223–24).

20. Quoted in Reiser, *Medicine and the Reign of Technology*, 167. Reiser notes that by the 1950s lab procedures took over much of the diagnostic work of the physician, further denying contact.

21. Regarding Stein's writing, Williams notes: "It is a valuable record. It permanently states that writing to be of value to the intelligence is not made up of ideas, emotions, data, but of words in configurations fresh to our senses" (*EK* 17).

22. J. Hillis Miller's *Poets of Reality* is the clearest statement of this perspective on Williams's work. Joseph Riddel is correct in his assertion that Williams was not trying to reestablish an ontological connection between words and things (*Shaken Realist*), but he underestimates the importance for Williams of the word's ability to confront and re-present a pathological materiality.

7. *Public Health, Plague, and Apocalypse*

1. Quoted in Rosenberg, *Cholera Years*, 148.

2. Quoted in Brandt, *Bullet*, 23.

3. Ramazzini, *Diseases of Workers*, 13.

4. Today the middle class is increasingly exposed to hazards in the workplace including such problems as the computer VDU and sealed-building toxic exposure.

5. Chadwick, *Report*, 86.

6. Ibid., 84.

7. Ibid., 93.

8. Ibid., 98.

9. Dix, "Memorial," 3.

10. Ibid., 4.

11. Ibid., 15.

12. Ibid., 16.

13. Few nineteenth-century American hospitals admitted alcoholics or syphilitics, and when they did, they charged higher rates (Rosenberg, *Care of Strangers*, 23, passim). The regulations of Massachusetts General (1861) read: "Persons infected with Syphilis shall not be admitted, except by vote of the Board of Trustees, and when admitted, shall pay not less than double the usual rates of board" (41).

14. *Massachusetts General Hospital By-laws, Rules and Regulations*, 43.

15. Quoted in Brandt, *Bullet*, 134.

16. Le Corbusier, *Toward a New Architecture*, 277.

17. In order to curb the incidence of VD during World War I, J. Frank Chase of the New England Watch and Ward Society argued for the establishment of the Army Corps of Moral Engineers (Brandt, *Bullet*, 73).

18. Doctor MacFarland in Williams's "Hands across the Sea"—an ex-soldier and physician working in public health for the League of Nations—comments on the "incredible stupidities of peoples" he is sent to help (*FD* 16).

19. Mansfield Merriman, whose sanitary-engineering textbook Williams used at the University of Pennsylvania Medical School, sums up the prevailing attitude toward the effects on the poor of a breakdown in sanitation: "the inhabitants of a community whose streets, houses, and persons are unclean usually do not have as nourishing food, systematic exercise, and refreshing sleep as those who live under good hygienic conditions" (*Elements of Sanitary Engineering*, 23–24).

20. Osler, *Principles and Practice of Medicine*, 267.

21. Merriman, *Elements*, 7.

22. Foucault has traced the expanded authority of the physician in determining insanity *(Madness and Civilization)*, the seat of disease *(The Birth of the Clinic)*, criminality *(Discipline and Punish)* and sexual deviance *(The History of Sexuality)*.

23. Williams, "The Doctor," 35.

24. Mariani, *New World*, 187, 91.

25. Brandt, *Bullet*, 157–59.

26. Published in the *William Carlos Williams Review* 9.1–2.

27. This comment recalls the early poem "Ogre," where the poet's thoughts about a "little girl with well-shaped legs . . . would / burn [her] to an ash" (*CP1* 95).

28. Thucydides, "Pestilence," 98.

29. Ibid., 101.

30. For example, because of the mass mobilization of soldiers during World War I and the occurrence of VD in epidemic proportions, public health workers were able to institute broad legislative reforms and command fairly large budgets (see Brandt, *Bullet*, chapter 2).

31. Merriman, *Elements*, 12–13.

32. Girard, "Plague in Myth and Literature," 512.

33. For example, Defoe's narrator spends considerable time marveling at the efficacy of public measures and the relative economic health of London.

34. Girard, "Plague in Myth and Literature," 512.

35. And their marital difficulties; see Mariani, *New World,* 285.

36. This writing as therapy takes the form of a perceptual apocalypse: "To have nothing in my head."

37. One of the most famous in medical history is Ulrich von Hutton's classic description of syphilis, a disease from which he suffered.

38. "The Late Singer" is usually read as a poem commenting on Williams's sense of belatedness—lack of publishing success, etc. It is also of significance because it was written near the end of the 1918-19 flu epidemic documented by "January"; consequently, it is a celebration of rebirth and an emergence from a period of time lost through overwork.

39. Military metaphors proliferate in medicine, both in describing the action of disease and in therapeutics. Susan Sontag notes this phenomenon in *Illness as Metaphor* (64), as does Fleck in a discussion of immunology (*Genesis,* 55). In World War I the Civilian Committee to Combat Venereal Disease distributed a flyer that read: "In a modern battle the artillery clears the way. After the Big Guns comes the individual effort—the bayonet charge, the hand-to-hand conflict. The way is being cleared to attack the venereal disease problem" (Brandt, *Bullet,* 78). In the United States the Public Health Service is organized on a military model, led by the surgeon general.

40. Quoted in Clendening, *Source Book,* 616.

41. As the various proponents of "Gaia" theory argue. See, for example, the recent work of Lynn Margulis. Mansfield Merriman often distinguishes between "good" and "bad" bacteria as if this were an unproblematic category.

42. Paul Mariani notes that "'Asphodel' is Williams' closest approximation to the apocalyptic genre" (*New World,* 671), but elements of apocalypse are frequent in many of his texts. See, for example, *Kora in Hell, Last Nights of Paris* (a translation of Philippe Soupault's *Les dernieres nuits de Paris*), "Portrait of the Author," "Burning the Christmas Greens," "A Morning Imagination of Russia," and the great fire in *Paterson.*

8. Paterson, *Placebos, and Postmodernism*

1. Almost a century earlier, Oliver Wendell Holmes had advocated pitching the entire materia medica into the sea: "all the better for mankind,—and all the worse for the fishes" ("Currents and Counter-currents in Medical Science," *Medical Essays,* 203).

2. Gold, "Placebos," 1721.

3. Ibid., 1722.

4. "I have no more difficulty coming to terms with the use of sugar of milk which I know has only psychotherapeutic values, than with the use of elixir of iron, quinine, and strychnine as a 'tonic.' The latter has all the support of traditional misinformation, but not a vestige of scientific evidence" (Ibid., 1726).

5. Ibid., 1719.

6. Jameson, *Postmodernism,* xxii.

7. Baudrillard, *Simulations,* 5.

8. Ibid., 153.

9. Le Corbusier, *Toward a New Architecture*, 62.

10. Jameson, *Postmodernism*, 2. He discusses Le Corbusier (and Manfredo Tafuri's critique of modernism, *Architecture and Utopia*) and the politics of space in "Architecture and the Critique of Ideology," in *Ideologies of Theory*, vol. 2.

11. Jameson sees in the disappearance of the "great writer" another sign of postmodernism's denial of hierarchy (*Postmodernism*, 306–7).

12. Surman, "Toward the Crystal," 187.

13. Given Williams's indictment of the austerity of the Puritans in *In the American Grain*, it is somewhat surprising that he maintained his allegiance to the crystal, particularly as it is embodied in International-Style architecture. In Le Corbusier's *Toward a New Architecture*, austerity and purity become clear moral values. In a sense, his attack on the Puritans show his early doubts about the modernist project as manifested in the "crystal."

14. In *William Carlos Williams: The Later Poems* Jerome Mazarro argues that Williams returned to the image of the crystal in the poems collected with the Brueghel sequence (175). Mazarro includes as an example, however, "He Has Beaten about the Bush Long Enough," which ends with "the crystal- / line pattern / of // new ice on / a country / pool" (*CP2* 405). In Williams's early work the image of the crystal was nearly always positive (In *Spring and All* "Poetry has to do with the crystallization of the imagination" [*CP1* 226]), but in this poem he uses it to describe the mind of a young critic (Edwin Cady) who has attacked both Mary Ellen Solt's presentation of her work on Williams and Williams's own work. The "crystal- / line pattern" described in this poem is hardly the crystal of the imagination.

15. The tie between the prism and Williams's father is even tighter when one compares the opening lines of Moore's poem—"not in the days of Adam and Eve but when Adam / was alone"—to Williams's own 1936 poem on his father entitled "Adam" and set in an "eden"—the Caribbean.

16. The reference to Darwin in "Asphodel" is significant, since *Origin of Species* is the embodiment of nineteenth-century science's quest for the center, or in this case the originating moment of history from which springs today's species. It is an etiological model of truth.

17. Williams's essay "The Poem as a Field of Action" celebrates production for production's sake. As Jean Baudrillard and Walter Benjamin ("Art in the Age of Mechanical Reproduction") have shown, profusion also subverts origin or first cause.

18. Jameson, *Postmodernism*, 64.

19. Jameson also draws a clear distinction between postmodern pastiche and high modernist collage along similar lines (*Postmodernism*, 17).

20. Donley refers to Lee Schultz's 1977 dissertation as support for her discussion ("Relativity and Radioactivity in William Carlos Williams' *Paterson*," 7).

21. Paul Mariani notes that Williams saw the film in March or April 1944 and it "provided him with his radiant image" (*New World*, 492). In *Paterson* the lines "The radiant gist that / resists the final crystallization" (109) clearly refer to Madame Curie's radium. The words "final crystallization" occur in both the book and the film.

22. She shows many of the signs of the alternative to the masculine model of scientific practice proposed by Keller in her *A Feeling for the Organism: The Life and Work of Barbara McClintock*.

23. Friedman and Donley, *Einstein as Myth and Muse*, 69–70, and Steinman, *Made in America*, 67–68.

24. In different terms, Henry Sayre makes a similar point, arguing that the poems of what he calls Williams's middle years are either "visual" or "visionary" (*Visual Text*, 73–74).

25. Also, as Friedman and Donley caution, "relativity still describes a completely knowable, causal universe" (*Einstein*, 111), so it is not entirely incompatible with a nineteenth-century scientific epistemology. In "The Poem as a Field of Action" Williams stresses the speed-of-light constant—a point that provides relativity with a foundation: "Einstein had the speed of light as a constant—his only constant—What have we?" (*SE* 286). On this issue, see Bruno Latour, "A Relativistic Account of Einstein's Relativity."

26. Although he had not read Steinmetz at the time, the following would surely have appealed to Williams, focusing as it does on local perceptions but including the idea of energy rather than stable objects: "All that we know of the world is derived from the perceptions of our senses. They are the only real facts; all things else are conclusions from them. All sense perceptions are exclusively energy effects. That is, energy is the only real existing entity, the primary conception, which exists for us because our senses respond to it" (*Four Lectures*, 23). By the time he wrote "The Poem as Field of Action," he had read Steinmetz, whose definition of *field* is appropriate: "The energy field is a storage of energy in space, characterized by the property of exerting a force on any body susceptible to this energy" (*Four Lectures*, 46).

27. Rather than simply viewing Whitehead as a source of Williams's knowledge of relativity, it would perhaps be better to examine his fusion of the vitalist and mechanist models of the nineteenth century into his organicism—a move that has significance in both philosophy and science (see, for example, Donna Haraway's *Crystals, Fabrics, and Fields: Metaphors of Organicism in Twentieth-Century Developmental Biology*). Whitehead's organicism is closely related to the numerous scattered and, at times, incoherent statements Williams made throughout his career on the role of the "imagination."

28. There the belated influence of Steinmetz can be seen, particularly in the final lecture, "Characteristics of Space."

29. Sayre, *Visual Text*, 111.

30. Riddel's discussion of Curie in *The Inverted Bell* (241–47) works through these same issues from a Derridian perspective, coming to many of the same conclusions. Also see Walter Scott Peterson on Williams's chemistry, *An Approach to Paterson*, 195–99.

31. Paul Bove, "The World and Earth of William Carlos Williams: *Paterson* as a 'Long Poem,'" 592.

32. Diggory, *Ethics of Painting*, 61.

33. Mazzaro also discusses the "relativity" of this poem (*Later Poems*, 84–85).

34. The poems written in the triadic line or the variable foot (which he defined in terms of relativity) create a more reflective tone simply because they must be read slowly.

35. See "Transitional" and the Marsden letters in *The Egoist.*

36. I must stress Williams's shifting attitudes in this period. He can surrender his power to the female principle in one breath and then turn around to write the following 1952 letter: "I must make the new meter out of whole cloth, I've got to know the necessity back of it. I am not driven by the search for personal distinction, I don't want to appear in person. But I want to see the unknown shine, like a sunrise. I want to see that overpowering mastery that will inundate the whole scene penetrate to that last jungle" (*SL* 313). Rather than seeing his shifts as incoherent or inconsistent, they can be used as further evidence of a postmodern attitude. Like his poetic father Walt Whitman (another famous postmodernist?), Williams will contradict himself with little (overt) concern.

37. These lines call up his early *In the American Grain,* which depicts the Americas as a woman waiting to be defiled by the aggressive European explorers.

38. In 1946, when Williams received an honorary LL.D. from the University of Buffalo, he was on the same dais as Vannevar Bush, the director of the atomic bomb project (Mariani, *New World,* 533).

39. Some lines from *Paterson* can serve as a gloss on this passage as well as a commentary on an overly facile epistemology that equates clarity with plain speech or "direct apprehension of the thing":

> Clearly, they say. Oh Clearly! Clearly?
> What more clear than that of all things
> nothing is so unclear, between man and
> his writing, as to which is the man and
> which the thing and of them both which
> is the more to be valued.
>
> (*P* 116)

40. Perhaps a reference to Einstein's speed-of-light constant, which either keeps him in a stable epistemology (the speed of light is the one thing you can count on), or allows him a way out of rigidity to the more fluid, olfactory-invoked love.

41. In *William Carlos Williams and the Ethics of Painting* Terence Diggory argues that love rather than domination or authority is the primary attitude in the poems about Brueghel's "Adoration of the Kings." Diggory tends to see a continuity of that attitude throughout Williams career even though he discusses primarily the late poems. I agree that love, which is a social, communal act, denies authority or possession and instead creates a relation between people (Diggory quotes *Spring and All,* the "fraternal embrace, the classic caress of author and reader" [*CP1,* 178]), but would add that this attitude did not begin to play a major role in Williams's work until the late poems. The marriage theme is crucial in those poems because it carries with it a sense of self-abnegation. Regarding "Asphodel," Ann Fisher-Wirth has claimed, "In Williams' own self-conception, it seems as if his identity is absolutely tied to his being married—at times, in fact, as if he only began to exist when he got married. For him, to marry is to become present to the world, to engage in the world, to acknowledge and affirm the reality of existence" (*William Carlos Williams and Autobiography,* 131).

42. Munthe, *San Michel,* 32.

43. Ibid., 33. This passage is followed by Munthe's footnote: "Colitis, as this word is used now, was not known in those days. Many sins have been committed both by doctors and patients in the name of colitis during the early stage of its brilliant career. Even to-day there is not seldom something vague and unsatisfactory about this diagnosis."

44. Ibid., 39.

45. *Paterson*, book 5, ends with a famous image where "We know nothing and can know nothing . / but / the dance."

Bibliography

Abbott, A. C. *The Principles of Bacteriology.* 6th ed. Philadelphia: Lea Brothers, 1902.

[Arnauld of Villanova]. *De cautelis medicorum.* In *Henry E. Sigerist on the History of Medicine.* Edited by Felix Marti-Ibanez. New York: MD, 1960.

Aronowitz, Stanley. *Science as Power: Discourse and Ideology in Modern Society.* Minneapolis: University of Minnesota Press, 1988.

Baudrillard, Jean. *Simulations.* Translated by Paul Foss, Paul Patton, and Phillip Beitchman. New York: Semiotext(e), 1983.

Bell, Barbara Currier. " 'The Use of Force' and First Principles in Medical Ethics." *Literature and Medicine* 3 (1985): 143–51.

Benjamin, Walter. "The Work of Art in the Age of Mechanical Reproduction." In *Illuminations,* translated by Harry Zohn. New York: Harcourt, Brace & World, 1968.

Berliner, Howard. "Medical Modes of Production." In *The Problem of Medical Knowledge: Examining the Social Construction of Medicine.* edited by Peter Wright and Andrew Treacher. Edinburgh: Edinburgh University Press, 1982.

Bernard, Claude. *An Introduction to the Study of Experimental Medicine.* Translated by Henry Copley Green. New York: Dover, 1957.

Bleier, Ruth, ed. *Feminist Approaches to Science.* New York: Pergamon Press, 1988.

Boroff, Marie. "William Carlos Williams: The Diagnostic Eye." In *Medicine and Literature,* edited by Enid Rhodes Peschel and Neale Watson. New York: Academic Publications, 1980.

Bove, Paul. "The World and Earth of William Carlos Williams: *Paterson* as a 'Long Poem.' " *Genre* 11 (1978): 592.

Brandt, Allan M. *No Magic Bullet: A Social History of Venereal Disease in the United States since 1880.* New York: Oxford University Press, 1985.

Camus, Albert. *The Plague.* Translated by Stuart Gilbert. New York: Modern Library, 1948.

Chadwick, Edwin. *Report on the Sanitary Condition of the Labouring Popula-

Bibliography

tion of Great Britain. Edited by M. W. Flinn. Edinburgh: University of Edinburgh Press, 1965.

Charlotte Medical Journal 2.2 (April 1915).

The City. Directed by Ralph Steiner and Willard Van Dyke. Civic Films Inc., 1939.

Clendening, Logan, ed. *Source Book of Medical History.* New York: Dover, 1960.

Coles, Robert. *William Carlos Williams: The Knack of Survival in America.* New Brunswick, N.J.: Rutgers University Press, 1975.

Conrad, Bryce. "Engendering History: The Sexual Structure of William Carlos Williams' *In the American Grain.*" *Twentieth-Century Literature* 35.3 (Fall 1989): 254–78.

Corbusier, Le. *Towards a New Architecture.* Translated by Frederick Etchells. New York: Dover, 1986.

Curie, Eve. *Madam Curie.* Translated by Vincent Sheean. New York: Doubleday, Doran, 1938.

Cushman, Stephen. *William Carlos Williams and the Meanings of Measure.* New Haven, Conn.: Yale University Press, 1985.

DeBord, Guy. *The Society of the Spectacle.* Detroit: Black and Red, 1977.

Defoe, Daniel. *A Journal of the Plague Year.* Edited by Anthony Burgess and Christopher Bristow. London: Penguin Books, 1966.

Diggory, Terence. *William Carlos Williams and the Ethics of Painting.* Princeton, N.J.: Princeton University Press, 1991.

Dijkstra, Bram. *Cubism, Stieglitz, and the Early Poetry of William Carlos Williams: The Hieroglyphics of a New Speech.* Princeton, N.J.: Princeton University Press, 1969.

Dix, Dorothea L. "Memorial: To the Legislature of Massachusetts." In *On Behalf of the Insane Poor.* New York: Arno Press, 1971.

Donley, Carol C. "Relativity and Radioactivity in William Carlos Williams' *Paterson.*" *William Carlos Williams Newsletter* 5.1 (Spring 1979): 6–11.

Driscoll, Kerry. *William Carlos Williams and the Maternal Muse.* Ann Arbor, Mich.: UMI Research Press, 1987.

Duffey, Bernard. *A Poetry of Presence: The Writing of William Carlos Williams.* Madison: University of Wisconsin Press, 1986.

Eliot, Thomas Stearns. *Collected Poems, 1909–1962.* New York: Harcourt, Brace & World, 1970.

———. "Tradition and the Individual Talent." In *Selected Prose of T. S. Eliot,* edited by Frank Kermode. New York: Harcourt Brace Jovanovich, 1975.

Emerson, Haven. "The Protection of Health through Periodic Medical Examinations," *Journal of the Michigan Medical Society* 21 (1922): 399–403.

Feyerabend, Paul. *Against Method.* New York: Verso, 1978.

Fisher-Wirth, Anne. *William Carlos Williams and Autobiography: The Woods of His Own Nature.* University Park, Pa.: Pennsylvania State University Press, 1989.

Fleck, Ludwik. *The Genesis and Development of a Scientific Fact,* translated by F. Bradley and T. J. Trenn. Chicago: University of Chicago Press, 1979.

Flexner, Abraham. *Medical Education: A Comparative Study.* New York: Macmillan, 1925.

Bibliography

————. *Medical Education in the United States and Canada.* New York: The Carnegie Foundation for the Advancement of Teaching, 1910. Reprint. New York: Arno Press, 1972.

Foucault, Michel. *The Birth of the Clinic.* Translated by A. M. Sheridan Smith. New York: Vintage Books, 1975.

————. *Discipline and Punish: The Birth of the Prison.* Translated by Alan Sheridan. New York: Pantheon, 1977.

————. "The Discourse on Language." In *The Archaeology of Knowledge,* translated by A. M. Sheridan Smith. New York: Pantheon Books, 1972.

————. *The History of Sexuality,* vol. 1. Translated by Robert Hurley. New York: Random House, 1978.

————. *Madness and Civilization: A History of Insanity in the Age of Reason.* Translated by Richard Howard. New York: Random House, 1965.

————. *Power/Knowledge: Selected Interviews and Other Writings.* Edited by Colin Gordon. Translated Colin Gordon, Leo Marshall, John Mepham, and Kate Soper. New York: Pantheon Books, 1977.

Francis, Valentine Mott. *A Thesis on Hospital Hygiene.* New York: J. F. Trow, 1859.

Fried, Michael. *Realism, Writing, Disfiguration.* Chicago: University of Chicago Press, 1987.

Friedman, Alan J., and Carol C. Donley. *Einstein as Myth and Muse.* Cambridge: Cambridge University Press, 1985.

Giedion, Siegfried *Mechanization Takes Command.* London: Oxford University Press. 1948. (Reprint. New York: Norton, 1969).

Gilbert, Sandra M. "Purloined Letters: William Carlos Williams and 'Cress.'" *William Carlos Williams Review* 11.2 (Fall 1985): 5–15.

Girard, René. "The Plague in Literature and Myth." In *Contemporary Critical Theory,* edited by Dan Latimer. New York: Harcourt Brace Jovanovich, 1989.

Gold, Harry, et al. "The Use of Placebos in Therapy." *New York State Journal of Medicine* 46 (1946): 1718–27.

Green, Harvey. *The Light of the Home.* New York: Pantheon Books, 1983.

Haller, John S. *American Medicine in Transition, 1840–1910.* Urbana: University of Illinois Press, 1981.

Haraway, Donna Jeanne. *Crystals, Fabrics, and Fields: Metaphors of Organicism in Twentieth-Century Developmental Biology.* New Haven, Conn.: Yale University Press, 1976.

————. *Primate Visions: Gender, Race, and Nature in the World of Modern Science.* New York: Routledge, 1989.

Harding, Sandra. *The Science Question in Feminism.* Ithaca, N.Y.: Cornell University Press, 1986.

Hawthorne, Nathaniel. "The Birth-mark." In *Tales and Sketches,* edited by Roy Harvey Pearce. New York: Library of America, 1982.

Heidegger, Martin. *The Question Concerning Technology and Other Essays.* Translated by William Lovitt. New York: Harper & Row, 1977.

Hendricks, Gordon. *The Photographs of Thomas Eakins.* New York: Grossman, 1972.

Heseler, Baldasar. *Andreas Vesalius' First Public Anatomy at Bologna, 1540.* Edited by Ruben Eriksson. Stockholm: Almqvist & Wiksells, 1959.

Bibliography

Hirst, Barton Cooke. *A Text-Book of Obstetrics.* 7th ed. Philadelphia: Saunders, 1912.

Holmes, Oliver Wendell. "Currents and Counter-currents in Medical Science," In *Medical Essays, 1842–1882.* 4th ed. Boston: Houghton Mifflin, 1887.

Jacobus, Mary, Evelyn Fox Keller, and Sally Shuttleworth, eds. *Body Politics.* New York: Routledge, 1990.

Jameson, Fredric. "Architecture and the Critique of Ideology." In *Ideologies of Theory,* vol. 2. Minneapolis: University of Minnesota Press, 1988.

———. *Postmodernism; or, The Cultural Logic of Late Capitalism.* Durham, N.C.: Duke University Press, 1991.

Janowitz, Anne. *"Paterson:* An American Contraption." In *William Carlos Williams: Man and Poet,* edited by Carroll Terrell. Orono, Maine: National Poetry Foundation, 1983.

Johns, Elizabeth. *Thomas Eakins: The Heroism of Modern Life.* Princeton, N.J.: Princeton University Press, 1983.

Jordanova, Ludmilla. *Sexual Visions.* Madison: University of Wisconsin Press, 1989.

Journal of the Medical Society of New Jersey 9.11 (November 1914).

Journal of Nervous and Mental Disease 38 (1911).

Keller, Evelyn Fox. *A Feeling for the Organism: The Life and Work of Barbara McClintock.* New York: Freeman, 1983.

———. *Reflections on Gender and Science.* New Haven, Conn.: Yale University Press, 1985.

Kenner, Hugh. "A Note on *The Great American Novel." Perspective* 6.4 (Autumn 1953): 177–82.

Kern, Stephen. *The Culture of Time and Space, 1880–1918.* Cambridge, Mass.: Harvard University Press, 1983.

Knorr-Cetina, Karin D. *The Manufacture of Knowledge.* Oxford: Pergamon Press, 1981.

Koch, Vivienne. *William Carlos Williams.* New York: New Directions, 1950.

Kuhn, Thomas. *The Structure of Scientific Revolutions.* 2d ed. Chicago: University of Chicago Press, 1970.

Latour, Bruno. "Give Me a Laboratory and I Will Raise the World." In *Science Observed,* edited by K. Knorr and M. Mulkay. London: Sage, 1983.

———. "One More Turn after the Social Turn: Easing Science Studies into the Non-Modern World." In *Social Dimensions of Science.* South Bend, Ind.: University of Notre Dame Press, 1992.

———. *The Pasteurization of France.* Translated by Alan Sheridan and John Law. Cambridge, Mass.: Harvard University Press, 1988.

———. "Postmodern? No, Simply Amodern: Steps towards an Anthropology of Science." *Studies in the History and Philosophy of Science* 21 (1990): 145–71.

———. "A Relativistic Account of Einstein's Relativity." *Social Studies of Science* 18 (1988): 3–44.

———. *Science in Action.* Cambridge, Mass.: Harvard University Press, 1987.

Latour, Bruno, and Steve Woolgar. *Laboratory Life: The Construction of Scientific Facts.* Rev. ed. Princeton, N.J.: Princeton University Press, 1986.

Bibliography

Leavitt, Judith Walzer. *Brought to Bed: Childbearing in America, 1750–1950.* New York: Oxford University Press, 1986.

Lentricchia, Frank. "Patriarchy against Itself: The Young Manhood of Wallace Stevens." *Critical Inquiry* 13.4 (Summer 1987): 742–86.

Loeb, Harold. *Life in a Technocracy: What It Might Be Like.* New York: Viking Press, 1933.

Loevy, Steven Ross. "Introduction to William Carlos Williams's *Rome.*" *Iowa Review* 9.3 (Summer 1978): 1–65.

Lucic, Karen. *Charles Sheeler and the Cult of the Machine.* Cambridge, Mass.: Harvard University Press, 1991.

Ludmerer, Kenneth M. *Learning to Heal.* New York: Basic Books, 1985.

Lyotard, Jean-François. *The Differend.* Tr. Georges Van Den Abbeele. Minneapolis: University of Minnesota Press, 1988.

———. *The Postmodern Condition: A Report on Knowledge.* Translated by Geoff Bennington and Brian Massumi. Minneapolis: University of Minnesota Press, 1984.

MacGowan, Christopher J. *William Carlos Williams's Early Poetry: The Visual Background.* Ann Arbor, Mich.: UMI Research Press, 1984.

Madam Curie. Directed by Mervyn LeRoy. Metro-Goldwyn-Mayer, 1944.

Mariani, Paul. *William Carlos Williams: A New World Naked.* New York: McGraw-Hill, 1981.

Marling, William. "'Corridor to a Clarity': Sensuality and Sight in Williams' Poems." *Twentieth-Century Literature* 35.3 (Fall 1989): 285–98.

———. *William Carlos Williams and the Painters, 1909–1923.* Athens, Ohio: Ohio University Press, 1982.

Mason, William Pitt. *Water Supply.* New York: Wiley, 1916.

Massachusetts General Hospital By-Laws, Rules, and Regulations. Boston: Rand & Avery, 1861.

Mazzaro, Jerome. *William Carlos Williams: The Later Poems.* Ithaca, N.Y.: Cornell University Press, 1973.

Meikle, Jeffrey L. *Twentieth Century Limited: Industrial Design in America, 1925–1939.* Philadelphia: Temple University Press, 1979.

Merriman, Mansfield. *Elements of Sanitary Engineering.* New York: Wiley, 1898.

Miki, Roy. *The Prepoetics of William Carlos Williams: Kora in Hell.* Ann Arbor, Mich.: UMI Research Press, 1983.

Miller, J. Hillis. *The Poets of Reality.* Cambridge: Belknap Press, 1965.

Monteiro, George. "Doc Rivers, Rogue Physician." *William Carlos Williams Review* 17.2 (Fall 1991): 52–58.

Mullan, Fitzhugh. *Plagues and Politics: The Story of the United States Public Health Service.* New York: Basic Books, 1989.

Munthe, Axel. *The Story of San Michel.* New York: Dutton, 1930.

Nay, Joan. "William Carlos Williams and the Singular Woman." *William Carlos Williams Review* 11.2 (Fall 1985): 45–54.

Nightingale, Florence. *Notes on Hospitals.* London: Parker & Son, 1859.

Orwell, George. "How the Poor Die." In *The Orwell Reader.* New York: Harcourt Brace Jovanovich, 1956.

Bibliography

Osler, William. *The Evolution of Modern Medicine.* New Haven, Conn.: Yale University Press, 1921.

———. *The Old Humanities and the New Science.* Boston: Houghton Mifflin, 1920.

———. *The Principles and Practice of Medicine.* 8th ed. New York: Appleton, 1918.

———. *Selected Writings of Sir William Osler.* Edited by W. W. Francis et al. London: Oxford University Press, 1951.

Ozenfant, Amédée. *Foundations of Modern Art.* Translated by John Rodker. 1931. Reprint. New York: Dover, 1952.

Pacey, Arnold. *The Culture of Technology.* Cambridge, Mass.: MIT Press, 1984.

Pellegrino, Edmund D. "Introduction." In *Medicine and Literature,* edited by Enid Rhodes Peschel and Neale Watson. New York: Academic Publications, 1980.

Poirier, Suzanne. "The Physician and Authority: Portraits by Four Physician-Writers." *Literature and Medicine* 2 (1985): 21–40.

Perloff, Marjorie. "The Man Who Loved Women," *Georgia Review* 34.4 (1980): 840–53.

———. *The Poetics of Indeterminacy.* Princeton, N.J.: Princeton University Press, 1981.

———. "Violence and Precision: The Manifesto as Art Form." *Chicago Review* 34.2 (Spring 1984): 65–99.

Peterson, Walter Scott. *An Approach to "Paterson."* New Haven, Conn.: Yale University Press, 1967.

Pinel, Philippe. *The Clinical Training of Doctors.* Edited and translated by Dora B. Weiner. Baltimore: Johns Hopkins University Press, 1980.

Pound, Ezra. *Literary Essays.* Edited by T. S. Eliot. New York: New Directions, 1935.

Ramazzini, Bernardino. *Diseases of Workers.* Translated by Wilmer Cave Wright. New York: Hafner, 1961.

Reiser, Stanley Joel. *Medicine and the Reign of Technology.* Cambridge: Cambridge University Press, 1978.

Riddel, Joseph N. *The Inverted Bell: Modernism and the Counterpoetics of William Carlos Williams.* Baton Rouge: Louisiana State University Press, 1974.

———. "The Wanderer and the Dance: Williams Carlos Williams' Early Poetics." In *The Shaken Realist,* edited by Melvin J. Friedman and John B. Vickery. Baton Rouge: Louisiana State University Press, 1970.

Risse, Guenter B. "From Horse and Buggy to Automobile and Telephone: Medical Practice in Wisconsin, 1948–1930." In *Wisconsin Medicine: Historical Perspectives,* edited by Ronald L. Numbers and Judith Walzer Leavitt. Madison: University of Wisconsin Press, 1981.

Rosenberg, Charles E. *The Care of Strangers.* New York: Basic Books, 1987.

———. *The Cholera Years.* Chicago: University of Chicago Press, 1962.

Rouse, Joseph. *Knowledge and Power: Toward a Political Philosophy of Science.* Ithaca, N.Y.: Cornell University Press, 1987.

Bibliography

Rush, Benjamin. *Selected Writings.* Edited by Dagobert D. Runes. New York: Philosophical Library, 1947.

Sayre, Henry M. "American Vernacular: Objectivism, Precisionism, and the Aesthetics of the Machine." *Twentieth-Century Literature* 35.3 (Fall 1989): 310–42.

———. *The Visual Text of William Carlos Williams.* Urbana: University of Illinois Press, 1983.

Schmidt, Peter. *William Carlos Williams, the Arts, and Literary Tradition.* Baton Rouge: Louisiana State University Press, 1988.

Shapin, Steven. "The House of Experiment in Seventeenth-Century England." *Isis* 79.298 (September 1988): 373–404.

Shapin, Steven, and Simon Schaffer. *Leviathan and the Air-Pump: Hobbes, Boyle, and the Experimental Life.* Princeton, N.J.: Princeton University Press, 1985.

Showalter, Elaine. *Sexual Anarchy.* New York: Viking Press, 1990.

Sontag, Susan. *Illness as Metaphor.* New York: Farrar, Straus & Giroux, 1978.

———. *On Photography.* New York: Farrar, Straus & Giroux, 1977.

Sorrentino, Gilbert. "Polish Mothers and 'The Knife of the Times.' " In *William Carlos Williams: Man and Poet,* edited by Carroll Terrell. Orono, Maine: National Poetry Foundation, 1983.

Soupault, Philippe. *Last Nights of Paris.* Translated William Carlos Williams. New York: Full Court Press, 1982.

Starr, Paul. *The Social Transformation of American Medicine.* New York: Basic Books, 1982.

Stearns, Harold E., ed. *Civilization in the United States.* New York: Harcourt, Brace, 1922.

Segal, Howard P. *Technological Utopianism in American Culture.* Chicago: University of Chicago Press, 1985.

Semmelweis, Ignaz. *The Etiology, Concept, and Prophylaxis of Childbed Fever.* Translated and edited by K. Codell Carter. Madison: University of Wisconsin Press, 1983.

Shryock, Richard H. *Medicine in America: Historical Essays.* Baltimore: Johns Hopkins University Press, 1966.

Steinman, Lisa M. *Made in America.* New Haven, Conn.: Yale University Press, 1987.

Steinmetz, Charles Proteus. *Four Lectures on Relativity and Space.* New York: McGraw-Hill, 1923.

Stengel, Alfred. *A Text-book of Pathology.* Philadelphia: Saunders, 1900.

Stewart, Rick "Charles Sheeler, William Carlos Williams, and Precisionism: A Redefinition," *Arts Magazine* 58 (November 1983): 100–114.

Surman, Diana Collecut. "Toward the Crystal: Art and Science in Williams' Poetic." In *William Carlos Williams: Man and Poet,* edited by Carroll F. Terrell. Orono, Maine: National Poetry Foundation, 1983.

Tapscott, Stephen. *American Beauty: William Carlos Williams and the Modernist Whitman.* New York: Columbia University Press, 1984.

———. "Williams, Sappho, and the Woman-as-Other." *William Carlos Williams Review* 11.2 (Fall 1985): 30–44.

Bibliography

Tashjian, Dikran. *William Carlos Williams and the American Scene, 1920–1940.* Berkeley and Los Angeles: University of California Press, 1978.

Terrell, Carroll, ed. *William Carlos Williams: Man and Poet.* Orono, Maine: National Poetry Foundation, 1983.

Thompson, E. P. "Time, Work-Discipline, and Industrial Capitalism." *Past and Present* 38: 56–97.

Thucydides. "The Pestilence at Athens." In *Greek Medicine,* edited by John Arthur Brock. New York: Dutton, 1929.

Tichi, Cecelia. *Shifting Gears: Technology, Literature, and Culture in Modernist America.* Chapel Hill: University of North Carolina Press, 1987.

Townley, Rod. "Bidding for Fame at 50: Williams' *Collected Poems, 1921–1931.*" In *William Carlos Williams: Man and Poet,* edited by Carroll F. Terrell. Orono, Maine: National Poetry Foundation, 1983.

———. *The Early Poetry of William Carlos Williams.* Ithaca, N.Y.: Cornell University Press, 1972.

Trachtenberg, Alan. *The Incorporation of America: Culture and Society in the Gilded Age.* New York: Hill & Wang, 1982.

Treichler, Paula A. "Feminism, Medicine, and the Meaning of Childbirth." In *Body Politics,* edited by Mary Jacobus, Evelyn Fox Keller, and Sally Shuttleworth. New York: Routledge, 1990.

Tyson, James. *The Practice of Medicine.* Philadelphia: Blakiston, Son, 1896.

Van Duyn, Mona. "To 'Make Light of It' as Fictional Technique." *Perspective* 6.4 (Autumn-Winter 1953): 230–38.

Virchow, Rudolf. "Cellular Pathology." In *Disease, Life, and Man,* translated by Lelland J. Rather. Stanford, Calif.: Stanford University Press, 1958.

Vogel, Morris J. *The Invention of the Modern Hospital: Boston, 1870–1930.* Chicago: University of Chicago Press, 1980.

Vogel, Morris J., and Charles E. Rosenberg, eds. *The Therapeutic Revolution: Essays in the Social History of American Medicine.* Philadelphia: University of Pennsylvania, 1979.

Von Hutton, Ulrich. "A Treatise on the French Disease." In *Classic Descriptions of Disease,* edited by Ralph Major. Springfield, Ill.: Thomas, 1932.

Wagner, Linda Welshimer. *The Poems of William Carlos Williams.* Middletown, Conn.: Wesleyan University Press, 1964.

———. *The Prose of William Carlos Williams.* Middletown, Conn.: Wesleyan University Press, 1970.

Warner, John Harley. *The Therapeutic Perspective.* Cambridge: Harvard University Press, 1986.

Weaver, Mike. *William Carlos Williams: The American Background.* Cambridge: Cambridge University Press, 1971.

Weininger, Otto. *Sex and Character.* New York: Putnam, n.d.

Welch, William Henry. *Papers and Addresses,* vol 3. Baltimore: Johns Hopkins University Press, 1920.

Whitehead, Alfred North. *Science and the Modern World.* New York: Free Press, 1967.

Williams, William Eric. "The Doctor." *William Carlos Williams Review* 9.1–2 (Fall 1983): 35–42.

Willms, Janice, and Henry Schneiderman. "The Ethics of Impaired Physicians:

Bibliography

Wolfe's Dr. McGuire and Williams's Dr. Rivers." *Literature and Medicine* 7 (1988): 123–31.

Wilson, Richard Guy, Dianne H. Pilgrim, and Dickran Tashjian. *The Machine Age in America*. New York: Abrams, 1986.

Wright, Peter, and Andrew Treacher, eds. *The Problem of Medical Knowledge: Examining the Social Construction of Medicine*. Edinburgh: Edinburgh University Press, 1982.

Zukofsky, Louis. *Prepositions*. New York: Horizon Press, 1967.

———. " 'Recencies' in Poetry." In *An "Objectivists" Anthology*. New York: To Press, 1932.

Works by
William Carlos Williams

The Autobiography of William Carlos Williams. New York: New Directions, 1951.

"The Baroness Elsa Fretag von Loringhoven." *Twentieth-Century Literature* 35.3 (Fall 1989): 279–84.

The Build-Up. New York: New Directions, 1952. Reprint. 1968.

The Collected Poems of William Carlos Williams. Vol. 1, 1909–1939. Edited by A. Walton Litz and Christopher MacGowan. New York: New Directions, 1986.

The Collected Poems of William Carlos Williams. Vol. 2, 1939–1962. Edited by Christopher MacGowan. New York: New Directions, 1988.

Contact. New York, 1920–23. Reprint. New York: Klaus Reprint, 1967.

The Doctor Stories. Edited by Robert Coles. New York: New Directions, 1984.

The Embodiment of Knowledge. Edited by Ron Loewinsohn. New York: New Directions, 1974.

The Farmers' Daughters. New York: New Directions, 1961.

"The Great Sex Spiral: A Criticism of Miss Marsden's 'Lingual Psychology.'" *The Egoist* 4.3 (April 1917): 46 and 4.7 (August 1917): 110–11.

Imaginations. Edited by Webster Schott. New York: New Directions, 1970. Contains *Kora in Hell, Spring and All,* "The Descent of Winter," *The Great American Novel,* and *A Novelette and Other Prose.*

In the American Grain. New York: New Directions, 1956.

In the Money. Norfolk, Conn.: New Directions, 1940.

I Wanted to Write a Poem. Edited by Edith Heal. New York: New Directions, 1977.

Interviews With William Carlos Williams. Edited by Linda Wagner. New York: New Directions, 1976.

Last Nights of Paris, by Philippe Soupault. Translation. New York: Full Court Press, 1982.

"The Little Red Notebook." *William Carlos Williams Review* 9.1–2 (Fall 1983): 1–34.

Many Loves and Other Plays. New York: New Directions, 1961.

Works by William Carlos Williams

"Men . . . Have No Tenderness." *New Directions* 7 (1942): 426–36.

Others: A Magazine of the New Verse. 1915–19. Reprint. New York: Klaus Reprint, 1967.

Paterson. New York: New Directions, 1958.

A Recognizable Image: William Carlos Williams on Art and Artists. Edited by Bram Dijkstra. New York: New Directions, 1978.

"Rome." Edited by Steven Ross Loevy. *Iowa Review* 9.3 (Summer 1978): 1–65.

Selected Essays of William Carlos Williams. New York: New Directions, 1968.

The Selected Letters of William Carlos Williams. Edited by John C. Thirwall. 1957. Reprint. New York: New Directions 1984.

A Voyage to Pagany. 1928. Reprint. New York: New Directions, 1970.

White Mule. 1937. Reprint. New York: New Directions, 1967.

William Carlos Williams/John Sanford: A Correspondence. Santa Barbara, Calif.: Oyster Press, 1984.

Yes, Mrs. Williams: A Personal Record of My Mother. 1959. Reprint. New York: New Directions, 1982.

Index

Index

Index

Index

Index

Index

Index

Index

Index